THE LOSS OF THE ENGLISH TRADER

Dedicated to
Signalman Edward Allen
who gave his life on Hammond Knoll

The immortal Henry Blogg

The Loss of the English Trader

RNLI COXSWAIN HENRY BLOGG'S TOUGHEST MISSION

Cyril Jolly

ACORN EDITIONS

By the same Author –

HENRY BLOGG OF CROMER
S.O.S. – THE STORY OF THE LIFEBOAT SERVICE
THE VENGEANCE OF PRIVATE POOLEY
THE SPREADING FLAME
HISTORY OF THE DEREHAM METHODIST CIRCUIT

Acorn Editions
8, Oak Street, Fakenham, Norfolk NR21 9DY

© Cyril Jolly 1981

First published 1981

ISBN: 0 906554 06 3

Designed and produced by Sharp Print Management, Fakenham, Norfolk
Printed by NENE LITHO
Bound by WEATHERBY WOOLNOUGH

Contents

		Page
	Introduction	vii
CHAPTER 1	The Armed Freighter and her Gunner	1
2	The Beginning of the End	10
3	Aground on Hammond Knoll	19
4	Three Men Swept Overboard	29
5	'Lifeboat on the Way'	37
6	'Knockdown'	47
7	The Yarmouth and Gorleston Lifeboat Launches	56
8	Another Night on the Wreck	68
9	Rescued	73
	Epilogue	84
	Notes	95

Acknowledgements

I wish to thank William Hickson for the account of his experiences on the *English Trader;* Henry 'Shrimp' Davies, ex-coxswain of the Cromer lifeboat, and George Mobbs, ex-coxswain of the Yarmouth and Gorleston lifeboat for their stories of the mission, and the Royal National Lifeboat Institution for their invaluable help with official reports of the rescue.

Gressenhall   Cyril Jolly
NORFOLK
1981

List of Illustrations

Frontispiece
The immortal Henry Blogg

Page 39
Above, the *English Trader* lying in anchor in Havana, Cuba. Below, diagram of the layout of the *English Trader*.

Pages 40 & 41
The death throes of the *English Trader,* taken from the lifeboat as the crew left their stricken ship.

Page 42
Above, the Cromer lifeboat, the *H.F. Bailey*. Below the Yarmouth and Gorleston lifeboat, the *Louise Stephens.*

Page 77
The Cromer lifeboat, the *H.F. Bailey,* approaching the *English Trader* early on Monday morning when the seas had somewhat abated, to make the rescue of the crew. This picture was taken from the freighter by the 4th Engineer.

Page 78
The Cromer lifeboat crew, photographed after a mission in 1939. Left to right, G. Cox, R. Cox, J.R. Davies, J.J. Davies Jnr., W.H. Davies, J.J. Davies Snr., H. Blogg, J.W. Davies, H.T. (Shrimp) Davies, F. Davies, R.C. Davies, W.H. Davies.

Page 79
Above, top left: Cromer cox'n Henry Blogg. Top right: Gun layer William Hickson. Below left: George Mobbs, who was the Yarmouth and Gorleston lifeboat mechanic in 1941. Below right: Henry 'Shrimp' Davies of the Cromer lifeboat talking to Robert Cross of the Humber lifeboat at Spurn Point in the 1960's.

Page 80
Two photographs to illustrate conditions at sea – top, the Yarmouth and Gorleston lifeboat leaving harbour and below, the *H.F. Bailey* launching at Cromer.

PICTURE CREDITS

Introduction

 THIS IS the story of how a gallant, but somewhat temperamental 'lady' of the Merchant Navy, the *English Trader*, met her end, not at the hands of the Germans but of an older enemy – the sea. She had survived two years of war hazards; mines, torpedoes and bombs; sailed many thousands of miles (including 3,000 with all her four coal-filled holds on fire) and fetched and carried thousands of tons of valuable cargo to her U-boat threatened island home. It also tells what the crews of two Royal National Lifeboat Institution lifeboats risked and suffered to rescue forty-four of her crew from the fury of the North Sea in what Cromer's ex-coxswain Henry 'Shrimp' Davies now describes as 'the most thrilling mission' of his experience.

This mission was to test the seamanship and character of Cromer's famous coxswain, Henry Blogg, to the limit, but he survived the ordeal of near disaster and served another six years before retiring. He died in 1954.

The Institution's Chief Inspector, Commander T G Michelmore said of him: 'He was . . . a magnificent seaman of very few words with the courage of a lion; a man of quick decisions and resolute action, sparing neither himself, his crew, nor the lifeboat in taking grave risks to rescue unfortunate seamen faced with disaster. He always succeeded and always beat the fury of the gale.'

The service to the *English Trader* was his supreme trial, and the sea almost beat him. As Henry Blogg himself said when the lifeboat was 'knocked down', 'The boat was hit hardest abaft the fore cockpit. Had she been hit as hard along her whole length there would be no lifeboat crew in Cromer today.' But the boat did right herself and Henry Blogg finished the job.

CHAPTER 1
The Armed Freighter and her Gunner

 IN THE middle of October 1941, the *English Trader* was tied up at the Tate and Lyle wharf in London Docks and began unloading her cargo of sugar. She had picked up the valuable commodity in Cuba, and brought it back across the North Atlantic. It had been an eventful and costly voyage. Having loaded the sugar she went to Havana for engine repairs and then steamed up to St Johns in Newfoundland, which the Royal Canadian Navy had just made a base for its convoy Escort Force. The *English Trader* joined an eastward bound convoy of some thirty ships with destroyer escort. It was intensely cold and the steamer was festooned with icicles from every rail and wire when she set out for Greenland hoping that by steaming so far north the active U-boats might be avoided. They might also gain protection from air bases which the United States had recently opened there for convoy protection. But it was in vain.

After a lull in July and August following the loss of three U-boat aces in March, the U-boats were again inflicting awful loss on our merchant shipping. Britain needed 125 freighters into her ports every week to meet her barest demands. Although the convoy system was being steadily improved throughout 1941 and the use of ASDIC and high-frequency direction finding was giving the escorts greater opportunity to locate the submerged U-boats, the initiative was still with the enemy, for the introduction of U-boat 'wolf pack' tactics was most successful.

Two days out in the Atlantic the *English Trader's* crew, padded with balaclavas and duffel coats, had been entertained by a fiery display of Northern Lights. The gun layer, William Hickson, had left his gun-deck one night soon afterwards to take a mug of hot tea in the engineers' mess, when he heard the 'twang' of torpedoes hitting ships in the convoy. The vibrations of the exploding missiles travelled through the water and could actually be felt by surrounding ships. He rushed up to his gun-deck, putting on his steel helmet as he ran, and joining the other gunners on watch, he saw the whole ocean lit up by the lurid glare of blazing oil tankers. Pillars of flame and smoke leapt high into the dark, casting a blood-red light on the clouds and nearby ships. It was a sight almost as grand as nature's display and certainly more awe-inspiring to the sailors. The gunners stared in shocked silence watching the ghastly flare with the chilling knowledge that the sinister killers were still there and any moment might see the white and phosphorescent wake of a torpedo heading towards them.

The escorting destroyers were dashing about like worried sheepdogs round a mauled flock. But the submarines had stolen into the midst of the convoy in the darkness and were relatively safe from attack. Ship after ship was hit during the course of that fearsome night. At this period of the Battle of the Atlantic, the third phase of which had begun in March 1941, the escort group of a convoy was so weak that the task of protecting a fleet of ships spread out in two columns perhaps eight miles long, was an impossibility against a determined U-boat attack. Yet discipline held and the ships sailed determinedly on. That takes some doing when the ship immediately ahead is hit and stops dead beneath a pall of black smoke!

The Commodore of the convoy urgently called for increased speed. It was an eight-knot convoy and that was thought to be the *English Trader's* maximum speed. However, on receiving the signal, Captain Grimstone called his chief engineer and asked if he could possibly get any more from the ship. An hour or so later, on his way to the bridge, William Hickson, who had been on the *English Trader* since January 1940, was passing the fiddley (entrance to the stokehold), when he stopped suddenly for he saw a sight that astonished him. He went to the captain and told him what he had seen. Both men went back to look down into the boiler room. Captain Grimstone's face was a study of surprise as he exclaimed: 'I should never have believed it. No, not in a thousand years!'

Most of his firemen had given him repeated trouble since they had been signed on for this voyage. In Cuba, there had been so much fighting and drinking that several of them were put ashore and imprisoned until the freighter sailed. The captain averred they were some of the roughest characters sailing the seven seas, but on looking down into the stokehold he saw another aspect of these men. There were nine men, the entire fireman crew, working like demons to get every possible ounce of steam from the ship. The furnace doors were being flung open and the stokers almost engulfed as the flames leapt out at them when they shovelled in more coal. Stripped to the waist, shining with sweat, they rushed back and forth with barrow-loads of coal to feed the roaring furnaces. Three men only should have been there, the others were supposed to be resting, but at the engineer's request, every man had turned out and somehow managed to get almost ten knots from the ship to keep up with the rest of the convoy. One stoker suddenly looked up and saw the captain looking down into the stokehold. He waved his shovel cheerily, the sweat streaming down his face and body and cried: 'Hi, Captain!'

Captain Grimstone answered: 'I take off my hat to you,' and he did so! The next morning he had every fireman before him to thank him personally and give him a big helping of grog.

The much diminished but gallant convoy eventually made England and the *English Trader* steamed into London Docks.*

Having discharged her cargo on Thursday 23 October, the steamer began taking on a general cargo. General is the right word, for it included umbrellas, pocket watches, whisky, Andrews Liver Salts, farm tractors, agricultural implements, dresses and kitchenware. The newly-crated goods bore the proud slogan: 'BRITAIN DELIVERS THE GOODS', and it was a proud, defiant boast considering the murderous near-stranglehold the enemy was exerting now that the French Atlantic ports were in their possession. The goods were bound for Mombasa in Kenya, East Africa, but they never reached their destination, for, not the Germans, but the sea in a flaming temper, unloaded them three days later on Hammond Knoll, some twenty miles south-east of Cromer on the Norfolk coast.

Only eight members of the *English Trader's* old crew had been signed on for the fresh voyage when they returned from a seven days' leave. These were Captain Grimstone and his three deck officers; the mate (a Welshman); Arthur Lond, the second mate; and the third mate, John Elliott; also William Hickson, the gun layer, two gunners and the steward. The other 34 men who signed on in London were entirely new to the ship – sailors, firemen and engineers. The chief engineer, A. Berry, had just been promoted and this was his first ship as chief engineer. Arthur Lond and William Hickson had served longest with the ship, both having joined her in January 1940. John Elliott, the mate and the steward had joined soon after. Captain Grimstone had taken over command from Captain Harkness for the previous voyage. Whether or not the newness of the firemen and engineers to the ship led in any way to her death it is impossible to say, but events indicate that it might have done. It certainly did lead to some of the men being washed overboard after the vessel foundered.

Hitherto, the *English Trader* had been a fortunate ship. In her encounters with the enemy she had, in fact, inflicted more damage than she had herself received, but an incident happened on the Friday night in the London Docks which made some members of the crew feel uncomfortable. Most seamen have strong superstitions and this incident cast foreboding.

It seems that some of the dock workers, while loading the ship with her mixed cargo, had found between the winches a bottle of Jamaican rum, possibly left behind by the *English Trader's* previous crew. It is certainly unusual for sailors to overlook a bottle of rum, but in Cuba rum was cheap, strong and plentiful. There had been long bouts of drinking and fighting while the vessel was in port and some of the crew, particularly the firemen, had given much trouble. There is also the possibility that the bottle was part of the cargo and a case had been broached. In any case, three of the shore men proceeded to deal with the bottle. The Jamaican rum was strong enough to make one worker decide to stay on board when work stopped at about 6 pm. Some of the ship's gunners were on an anti-sabotage watch and other members of the crew were busy about their own concerns. No one took particular notice of the man when he stretched out on No 3 hatch which had already been loaded and covered. With his overcoat folded to form a pillow, the man settled down and was soon fast asleep. The night air was cold and damp, and nobody gave a thought to the sleeper on the hatch. Perhaps an occasional glance and a shrug of the shoulders, but on the whole, he was forgotten.

In the morning however, shortly after seven, as daylight came, he was seen to be lying still in the same position and when someone went to rouse the man to get him ashore, they discovered he was dead. He had died some time in the night from the effects of the rum and exposure.

With seagulls mewing about the ship as if in lament, the body was taken ashore for an inquest and a lot of questions were asked on the ship, but no blame could be attached to any member of the crew. Nevertheless, it was looked upon as a bad omen for ship and crew, making the *English Trader* a kind of hoodoo ship.

On Friday afternoon, October 24th, the *English Trader* was ready to sail, just waiting for the tide. A tug came alongside bringing the pilot. Gangways were hauled in. The mate was in the bows as 'anchor man', the second mate aft in charge of the stern mooring cable. Then with captain and pilot on the navigation bridge, orders were given: 'Let go for'ard.'

'Let go aft.'

Bells clanged, the engine-beat quickened and the freighter slipped from the quay, her screws churning the brown Thames water into a muddy froth, and her engine taking up a note of power, sent strong vibrations through the ship. The *English Trader's* last and fatal voyage had begun.

The new crew were unfamiliar as yet with their surroundings or some of the peculiarities of the ship. They were soon to learn of one peculiarity about their new vessel. Every ship has its character – even mass-produced Liberty ships. This individuality is not necessarily given by the builders. The *English Trader* was a 'character' of the sea. One of her eccentricities was an inability to maintain an even keel in the open sea for any length of time. Whether this was due in any way to her Arc form construction is not known*. A slight beam swell was enough to set her rolling to an uncommon degree. In rough weather a 30-degree roll was not unusual with her. In fact, on one occasion in the South Atlantic during a squall, she had neared the 45-degree mark with disastrous results to her port lifeboat which had been in the outslung position, as was usual in dangerous waters

*See Note 1, p 95

in wartime. The crew called her by a variety of names – none of them complimentary. Often, after joining a convoy, an escort, seeing her rolling, would steam up and demand what cargo she was carrying, possibly thinking she was carrying an awkward cargo such as torpedoes.

This had nothing to do with her end on Hammond Knoll, but it did make her an uncomfortable ship and many seamen were very glad to get off her. When she was in the mood, it was difficult to walk along her tilting, rolling decks and it would not do to leave a nearly full bucket of water about! The cook had many an exasperating experience with his half-full pots and pans.

Once, when William Hickson was on the gun-deck, he turned when he heard a terrific clatter and saw the cook standing in the doorway of the galley, red of face and swearing volubly. He had just flung a saucepan at the mast with all his force and this was quickly followed by others. He was mad with rage. The ship's steward had to go and pacify him with some rum and help him to clear up. William Hickson recalls that in his cabin he had a shelf of books on a bulkhead wall. It was fitted with a bar across the front to prevent books being dislodged, but in a heavy swell he had known the books to be pitched out over the retaining bar, so violent had been the movement of the *English Trader*. At times, the rails of the decks would dip in the water. She was a temperamental 'lady', yet, though many seamen cursed her, especially those newly joined, the men who got used to her ways allowed for her tantrums. The gun layer, for instance, aiming his guns when she was in a rolling carefree mood, would have fun turning the gun control handle to keep the target in his telescope. He had only seen one other ship with such a pronounced movement.

Leaving her berth at the Tate and Lyle wharf, the *English Trader* passed slowly downstream by the dock areas which resembled a forest of masts with ships and cranes, and warehouses teeming with activity for a couple of miles, till the open marshes were reached. The great cement works came and slid past, then Dartford and the ever-widening river. Little villages on the Kent and Essex side, fields and more marshes. Then the three training ships *Warspite, Worcester* and *Arethusa,* came one by one into view and dropped astern. Tilbury and more funnels and masts with a conglomeration of sheds and dock buildings. Until, late in the afternoon, the *English Trader* made Southend. Here the River Thames is wide enough for a convoy to form within the safety of the great boom before setting off for the far places of the world. The steamer dropped anchor in sight of the seaside resort's famous pier.

The pilot boat came alongside and took off the pilot. Captain Grimstone also went ashore to take part in the convoy conference and receive his sailing orders for the voyage. Having learned by bitter experiences of World War I, the convoy system was organised in 1939 at the outbreak of hostilities. Convoy Commodores were called in to command ocean-going convoys. They were mostly retired admirals, ageing but wise in the ways of the sea – and senior officers of the Merchant Navy. They selected a ship as their flagship for that journey, taking on board with them a Yeoman of Signals and a small signals staff. They had the very difficult task of keeping together a group of ships, varying greatly in size and speed, by night and day and co-operating with the escorting naval vessels when enemy action threatened their convoy.

The fall of France in June 1940 had virtually closed the English Channel to normal shipping convoys and after a disastrous attack in July 1940, by the enemy on Convoy OA178 off Portland, all ocean-going convoys from the Thames were routed up the East coast and round the North of Scotland. So Convoy EC90 had to sail north to the Firth of Forth before proceeding right round the North of Scotland to Oban and then on to Africa. This long detour (once made by the mauled Spanish Armada), was necessary.

Six Army gunners came on board at Southend to supplement William Hickson, the gun layer, and his four seamen-gunners. This brought the ship's total crew to 48 with a gun complement of 11. In addition, there were four seamen who had received training in gunnery. These seamen-gunners hurried to the gun-deck when needed. So the *English Trader* was up to full strength for her guns, and she needed to be for the enemy-haunted voyage up the East coast to Scotland and then over thousands of miles of ocean threatened by U-boats, German commerce raiders and Focke-Wulf Condors.

In the dawn's pallid light, on Saturday 25 October, the ships were keeping their allotted positions and the Commodore's flag, flying from the halyards of the leading freighter, gave the sailing signal. Each ship weighed anchor and began to move out in single line toward the gate of the boom which was open to let the convoy pass into the estuary and the North Sea.

There were about 30 ships, moving in single column through the narrow mineswept Channel. This number included over 20 ocean-going freighters, two or three coastal steamers and the two escorting destroyers, one of which was the ageing *HMS Vesper*. Once through the boom the ships formed into a double column. A light wind was blowing from the north-west; just enough to riffle the surface of the estuary. Visibility was fair to good and a blanket of cloud covered the sky at about 1200 feet. High over the convoy, making wide protective circles around the ships, were two fighter aircraft. Sharp young eyes looked down and scanned the grey sea, looking from that height like Morocco leather, searching for underwater tracks of the U-boats, while the unseen eyes of the radar shore station kept watch for signs of raiding enemy aircraft.

Convoy EC90 proceeded at a steady eight knots. For the *English Trader* this was nearing her maximum speed. She had little if any reserve, and her firemen were kept hard at it to hold her at this speed with a full head of steam. She was a coal burner, like most of the other ships in the group. Quite often, however, the difficulty of some small vessel caused the convoy speed to drop to seven knots or even six. This made it easier for the stokers of the freighter. The rest of the crew were active with their varying jobs, the duty signals staff being particularly busy for there was a constant interchange of messages between the Commodore's ship, his charges and the two escorting destroyers. Slowly, the new crewmen began finding their way about and learned some of the geography of their ship. There was no relaxing for those men on the bridge and gun-deck, they dared not relent in their watch, for this was the happy hunting ground of enemy raiders.

William Hickson had got out of his bunk at 6 am that morning and had spent almost all the rest of the day on the gun-deck. He was 'captain of the guns'. It was his responsibility to supervise their serviceability; the readiness of ammunition, the watches of gun crews as well as their welfare and discipline, and also flooding arrangements in the magazine.

Much of the story of what happened on the *English Trader* in the next 50 hours has been told by gun layer, William Hickson, this man had made the sea his life and served on numerous merchant ships before and throughout the six years of war. He is typical of the seamen who served and suffered untold hardships and misery, who died in their tens of thousands in keeping the sea-lanes of Britain open.

But before the outbreak of war in 1939, William Hickson took a job ashore; he also joined No 601 Squadron of the Royal Auxiliary Air Force as a rigger. So he was not surprised when, one morning in September 1939, he found two identical envelopes lying on his door-mat; one contained his call-up papers for the Royal Naval Reserve and the other for the Royal Air Force Volunteer Reserve! A tug-of-war had begun and he had to attend a Services Tribunal at Croydon.

After his case was set out before the tribunal a sharp discussion followed. But the Navy made out the stronger case and the President of the Court settled the matter by saying sharply: 'He's a sailor!'

William Hickson did not mind either way for he had found that although he enjoyed life in 601 Squadron, he had not really lost his love of the sea. At night lying in his warm bed, when the wind got up, whined and moaned as it did in the ship's rigging, he felt the old restless yearning to return to ships.

'I must have the sea in my blood,' he said. He would think of the times he stood on deck watching the stars winking and twinkling; the moonlight on rippling water and the dawn unfolding like a rose over a tropical sea. So he might as well accept the decision of the tribunal cheerfully.

The tribunal instructed him to report to *HMS President.* This was a training ship on the Thames Embankment and it is still used for training Royal Naval

Reserve personnel. Here, he was wisely advised by a Chief Petty Officer to volunteer as a gun layer. At the time, British merchant ships under great urgency were being armed as fast as equipment came along.

'It's the ideal job for you,' he said. 'You know the Merchant Navy and you'll be your own boss on board. That means a lot.'

So William Hickson volunteered and went to Shoeburyness for training and a final examination. He passed out as proficient and enrolled in the Defensively Equipped Merchant Service (DEMS) as a gun layer. He was paid by the Navy with a very small supplement from the vessel's owners.

On his gun-deck, the gun layer was in charge. Although he had to get an order from the bridge or ship's captain to open fire on surface craft, he could use his own discretion in firing at aircraft. The vessel's captain did not interfere with him. As he had been told, he would be 'his own boss'.

So William Hickson was detailed to his first ship as gun layer or gunner and one very bitter day in the severe January of 1940, he went by rail with three other young gunners to Hull to find his ship – the *English Trader*. They arrived at Hull Station at 4 am. It was snowing and the bleak, windswept streets were deserted. Everywhere was blacked out and closed. The young men were hungry, cold and a bit fed up. However, after wandering about for what seemed hours, they found a YMCA. It also was closed but a knock brought the warden to the door and soon he had them thawing out in front of a blazing fire. Then he hastily prepared a hot meal of eggs and bacon. William Hickson has had a soft spot for the YMCA ever since. After a wash and brush up the four grateful gunners left at 7.30 am to go to the naval depot and find their various ships.

William Hickson found the *English Trader*. She was being refitted for arming and was a mass of wiring. Timberwork was in progress building a gun-deck in the stern and cabins and quarters for the gun crew. When at last William Hickson was able to get on board he was delighted to find a four-inch breech-loading semi-automatic gun was being swung into position by a crane. He could scarce believe his good fortune, for he has since been assured that there were at that time only two of these advanced-type guns in the Merchant Navy – and he was to have one of them! The breech-loader in general use had, after firing, to be swabbed out with a mop and water by a member of the gun crew. This was to ensure no burning cordite was left in the barrel which might prematurely fire the next round. The semi-automatic therefore, was a great improvement for it was fitted with a swivelling tray which took both the shell and the cordite charge in a brass container, ejecting the charge case after firing. There was no need to swab out the barrel. The firing operation was simpler and much faster. In addition, the *English Trader* had a twelve-pounder anti-aircraft gun and a machine-gun. The gun-deck was aft and William Hickson had a cabin beneath it on the starboard side. The bo'sun and carpenter's cabins adjoined his, but they were on the port side.

Captain John Harkness commanded the ship. The first officer was a

Welshman who had been torpedoed on an earlier voyage and spent over thirty days in an open boat. Arthur Lond was second officer and also acted as unpaid gunnery officer. The third officer was a survivor from the *Titanic* disaster.

On 20th January 1940, they sailed out of the River Humber, escorting some unarmed French trawlers down to Southend. They soon found themselves in trouble for they ran into a British minefield and had to anchor and await a patrol boat to guide them out of it. From Southend they joined a large convoy bound for Freetown, and then, having loaded 7,000 tons of coal, they steamed independently across the South Atlantic to the River Plate.

On this voyage, the gun layer took the opportunity to train some of the seamen who had volunteered to help man the guns. He now looks back with pride on the fact that after the ship's bo'sun had made up a target raft which, with the ship steaming at eight knots, was dropped over the side; after several minutes gun drill and with the target now some four or five miles away, it was picked out with telescopic sights and fired at with 4in practice shells. There was only the flag attached to the mast to be seen but with the third round they hit the target. This greatly pleased everyone including Captain Harkness. Before firing the first round, the seaman-gunner with the telescope complained he could see nothing. William Hickson went over to him and found he still had the cap on the telescope! Hickson also recalls that in those early days of the war, he slept in pyjamas – but that luxury did not last long at sea as the war went on.

William Hickson remained with the *English Trader* during several adventurous voyages. When the vessel arrived in Leith in June 1941 Captain Harkness left her; he was being promoted to be master of the *Scottish Trader*.

CHAPTER 2
The Beginning of the End

 TO RETURN to Convoy EC90; as she approached the Barrow Deep, a narrow channel off the Essex coast, the 30 ships moved into single line astern with two fighter aircraft still spinning a protective web above the strung-out line of vessels. Their presence was a deterrent for any enemy aircraft.

With the Deep passed safely, the convoy re-formed into two columns and kept up a steady eight knots. The *English Trader* was placed well back in the port column, ahead of a ship of similar size and capacity, possibly carrying the same general cargo. But this did not mean that its maximum or economic speed was the same, or even the coal in her bunkers was the same – although she had taken it on at the same wharf. The weather was fine and dry, but it was overcast, as though rain was not far away.

The gun crews were wearing steel helmets as was customary when in action or on 'alert'. Normally they wore uniform or boiler suits: while the naval men, like William Hickson, wore their working suits, sou'westers and oilskins in bad weather, and when in really cold latitudes, balaclavas were the vogue. Duffel coats were usually worn in the night watches. Life-jackets of the Mae West type were always worn when on duty on deck, as were sea boots.

At this point of the voyage, the bo'sun fitted up a fog buoy to be ready in the event of fog descending quickly. After fastening one end of the cable to the stern mast, he carried it across the well-deck over the deck-house on the poop. The buoy was then ready to throw astern at a moment's notice. At the time, William Hickson thought nothing of this. It was standard procedure. He little guessed it was to be the means, some hours later, of saving his life!

The carpenter had finished his task of banging the wedges in the cleats around the hatch combings securing the tarpaulin covers. Dinnertime had come with the gun layer taking his meal hurriedly in the engineers' mess and the gunners in their mess room. No one tarried long over the meal for each man knew he might be needed at any moment on the gun-deck. They were too near 'Hitler's doorstep' to take things easy.

Captain Grimstone was on the bridge almost without a break. He paced from wing to wing or stopped for a minute or two and sat on a long-legged stool near the binnacle. From this position he could see the convoy spread out before him – a double line of dark-grey shapes on the grey October sea. His third officer, John Elliott, was with him much of the time and occasionally the two conversed on points arising from the progress of the ship and the substance of signals from the Commodore or from other ships.

William Hickson, long familiar with the *English Trader,* recalls that when standing on the gun-deck or any part of the after-deck, it was possible to know whether or not the engines were turning at full speed by listening to the sound of the screw. At top speed the sound was like a low-pitched humming-top; the hum rising and falling. The gunners called this hum her 'sing song'.

As was usual, the watch changed at midday – eight bells. It was the start of the second mate's watch. He was the ship's navigator and also acted as its unpaid gunnery officer. The latter job he took most seriously and never failed to keep William Hickson, as gun layer, informed of any developments affecting him and his job. There was a good understanding between them which kept a smooth liaison between gun-deck and bridge.

At about 1.30 pm when the afternoon watch was little advanced, the familiar 'sing song' of the engine gradually faded, changing to a quite different note. The bronze screw was turning noticeably slower. The gunners queried what was happening. There was no signal from the convoy Commodore instructing the ships to reduce speed and it was soon apparent that there was something amiss in the engine-room. The vessel began to lose way, seeming to slide astern and out of her position in the group, just as if she had suddenly become tired.

The crew on watch, of course, could not fail to notice it, but there were no immediate misgivings. To them it was just one of those things. They felt confident the Old Man knew what was happening and could handle the matter. They were not to know that this drop in engine revs was far more serious than they thought. It was, in fact, the beginning of the end.

The firemen on the afternoon watch increased their efforts, trying their hardest to make good the sluggishness of the engine. But they were unable to make up the loss of speed. The captain urgently summoned the chief engineer to the bridge and no doubt he received some sharp words from Captain Grimstone, who was quite capable of making himself clearly understood when occasion demanded. He would not be in a pleasant mood when he could see his ship lagging behind and losing her place in the group. She was the only ship in the convoy not keeping good station. He knew the capability of his ship although it was but his second voyage in her and he knew that the eight-knot speed of the convoy was not excessive for the *English Trader.*

At around two o'clock the vessel astern signalled her intention to overhaul the *English Trader* and take up a position ahead of her. This change brought up one of the two escorting destroyers, *HMS Vesper*, which hitherto had been steaming ahead on the starboard flank. Her Captain wanted to know what was happening and the cause of the trouble.

By 3 pm the ship was at least a half mile behind the rest of Convoy EC90 which steamed determinedly on and the outlook was beginning to look serious – German aircraft, U-boats or torpedo-boats relished finding a 'lame duck'. U-boats, in particular, like wolves, preferred to pick off stragglers. While she was with the other ships there was the protection of the two destroyers and the guns of the other freighters, but if she continued to drop further and further behind, this protection would be lost. The crew started to ask among themselves in subdued but somewhat worried tones, what the trouble could be and some sarcastic remarks were made about what was going on in the stokehold – for that was plainly where the trouble lay.

About this time the Commodore signalled *HMS Vesper* and she, in turn, slowed her engines and waited for the freighter to come abeam of her. Then her loud-hailer crackled instructions over the water: 'If you cannot regain your position by nightfall, you must make for harbour.'

At this, Captain Grimstone recalled the chief engineer to the bridge. He was very angry. He ordered his officer to get some men to the boilers who knew their job. He would listen to no excuses.

Unfortunately, at that moment, William Hickson came down the ladder from the 'Monkey Island' where he had been inspecting the four PAC (Parachute and Cable) rockets. The moment he set his foot on the navigating bridge the captain saw him and called: 'Will you come here a moment, Gunner?' Then he asked: 'You've been on this ship for a long time so tell me, have you ever seen it crawling along like this – or at any time lose its position in a convoy?

It was a direct question. The gun layer could not evade it. He suspected that Second Officer Lond had made some reference to him, as the captain and he had obviously been discussing the situation and Hickson, no doubt, rightly guessed that the second mate had said that the gunner would confirm his statements.

It was an embarrassing moment for the gun layer for he knew that the captain expected and would insist on a direct reply. He disliked imputing any blame to the engineers, but no attempt at evasion would do. He shook his head and replied: 'No, sir.'

Later he was able to confirm that Second Officer Lond had given his views after the captain had put a similar question to him. He too, had given the same reply as the gun layer. Nevertheless the fault was pointing to the chief engineer – who was doing his very best to find out what was wrong and to put it right.

The *English Trader* had coal-fired, forced-draught-feed boilers which meant that the fans boosting the draught of her boilers had to be precisely set. The chief engineer was new to the ship and, possibly, new to this type of firing.

Time dragged by and the *English Trader* with her 7,000 tons of assorted cargo rolled along in the wake of the main convoy, slipping further and further behind. And now there seemed little hope of regaining the protection of the group's massed guns – and the many eyes and ears that were alert for signs of hostile action.

The speed of the steamer at times dropped as low as four knots. The convoy was almost out of sight. The smudges of the many ships and the columns of smoke from the vessels steaming north showed faint against the horizon.

Towards evening the wind freshened and the sea grew choppy. The vessel was now well over two miles behind the last ship. The screw was turning sluggishly and the usual 'sing song' that William Hickson knew over the many thousands of miles he had sailed in her, was missing. All the frenzied efforts below in the stokehold were not stirring the ship to her accustomed rhythm.

No land was visible, but to the west was the Suffolk coast with its little holiday resorts of Aldeburgh and Southwold. Eastward, the grey waters of the North Sea stretched a hundred miles to Occupied Holland. The convoy was routed well to the east of the Scroby Sands. The Newark light vessel had gone, but ahead lay the buoys marking the safe channel, their lights winking as one by one, in turn, they appeared above the horizon. The navigating officer checked them as they passed. As the *English Trader* drew near to some, a mournful bell tolled its warning with the rolling of the waves, passing abeam and then the sad knell fading as they plugged on. Many green light buoys marking wrecks winked at them to port and starboard.

The gunners took their tea on the gun-deck in case of attack. Soon after, at about 5.30 pm, William Hickson was told by one of the seamen-gunners that the second mate wanted to see him on the bridge as quickly as possible. Knowing the seriousness of their situation, Hickson hurried off. He was not at all surprised to find Captain Grimstone waiting and also the chief and second mate. He assumed that the third mate was still at tea. He was.

Captain Grimstone did most of the talking. It was clear he was a worried man. He made various little quick gestures that betrayed his anxiety. He repeatedly insisted that the officers made personally sure there were no lights showing on the vessel after dark and that any man found smoking on the open decks should be reported to him immediately.

Turning to Hickson he said: 'Keep your chaps on their toes. We can expect air attack at any time. Don't wait for orders from the bridge. If you want any help let Mister Lond know.'

Unfortunately, the *English Trader*, like so many foreign-going ships, was not too well equipped with anti-aircraft weapons. Her main armament was the 4in semi-automatic which could only be used against surface craft. The 12-pounder, high and low angle, gun could be used against either air or surface attackers, but against aircraft its main purpose was to create a barrage using high explosive shells with pre-set fuses. These were set to detonate within the 3,000-feet range.

The object was to deter the enemy planes from flying through this barrage. At night, if this gun was to be used effectively, a lot depended on the weather conditions for the enemy had to be located quickly. On a dark night the gunners of merchant ships had to rely on their ears and they were lucky if they could spot an attacker before it was almost on top of them.

Beside the 12-pounder there were two Oerlikons (fitted in London just before this voyage) and four smaller machine-guns. Four PAC rockets were in their firing tubes on the Monkey Island. These rockets could destroy any low-flying aircraft which fell foul of their steel cables, suspended over the ship and held in position by the parachute. The firing lanyards for these rockets passed through the deck to hang just above the man at the wheel. He would pull the toggles when given the order from an officer on the bridge. When fired, the rockets reached about 200 feet.

Although there were eight gunners on the *English Trader* it took six of them to man the 12-pounder. It was usual, therefore, to call in an emergency, on some of the seamen who had previously received instruction in gunnery with the idea of reinforcing the guncrews. This practice was general in the Merchant Navy. It was so in the *English Trader*, and up to a month or so previously these seamen-gunners had made up the entire guncrew. Amateurs though they were, on the whole they were efficient and their enthusiasm almost brought them into line with the professionals.

On the laggard of Convoy EC90, every man on watch was alert. As the autumn daylight of this Saturday faded into dusk with a high three-quarters waxing moon blanketed by heavy clouds, the steel-helmeted gunners stood at their posts expecting trouble. A wind whistled a lament through the ship's rigging. The order had long been given to 'darken ship'. Deadlights were dropped and screwed home. Doorways were screeened. There was not a glimmer of light to be seen on the ship; the outline of her superstructure was dark in the deepening darkness. Men were shapes without faces. No one dared to strike a match for their own safety, quite apart from the captain's stern warning. With deadlights clamped down and blackout curtains carefully pulled and checked the steamer moved almost ghost-like northwards into the night, dragging her keel five miles behind the convoy.

The dull 'thud-thud' of the labouring screw sounded above all other noises but gradually the note changed a little – it was turning faster as if the severe words of the master and the efforts of firemen and engineers were having some result. The gunners heard it reach the usual 'sing-song'. It was a comforting sound as was the ever-present rush and hiss of the ship's wake and the familiar noises of waves as they met the grey hull and rebounded. Perhaps the ship could make up some of the leeway. But unfortunately the revival of the engines did not last long.

Then, abruptly, the pattern of familiar sounds was broken when from the convoy, now far ahead and quite unseen, came the dull boom of gunfire, and into the night sky went up a vivid curtain of red tracer bullets and exploding shells. The northern sky was slashed with streaks of lights, almost resembling a firework display. The convoy was under attack and was snarling back at the intruder like a bad-tempered yard-dog. The rumbles of bombs exploding in the water travelled through the sea to the straggler. The crew of the *English Trader* actually felt the bombs being dropped near the convoy. They were ominous noises that seemed to clutch at a man's stomach for the men of the lone freighter knew they were denied the massed fire-power of the convoy's guns. They would be near-naked in the face of a determined air attack.

The gunfire ceased almost as a conductor stops his players at a rehearsal. The darkness closed in again over the troubled ships ahead. But against the background noises of ship and sea the enemy aircraft could be heard still, somewhere in the clouds trying to dodge any moonlit patches. It was now looking around for an easier target, being intimidated by the convoy's spite. The half-veiled moon was reflected by the restless waters but the soft light it gave, rippling and dancing with the waves, was of little help to the tense waiting sailors.

Then, over the sound of wind and wave and the vibration of the engines came a new sound – a sound like a faint, singing whistle – such as the wind makes through telegraph wires on a lonely country road. Out of the darkness rushed the huge shape of a Dornier bomber, power-gliding at little more than mast height. Its black wings seemed to overshadow the ship like a fearsome bird of prey. Even through the gloom it was possible for the seamen to see two bombs fall from the aircraft's belly and plummet downwards. To an experienced bomb-aimer the ship presented a gift target – too close and too big to miss. The Germans had achieved complete surprise and there was no opposition – until possibly the most critical moment when the bomb-aimer's finger was about to press the release button. Then the *English Trader's* gunners opened fire.

One of the Army lance-corporals was holding a Lewis gun. It was ready to fire. As the twin-engined Dornier swooped at them, William Hickson grabbed the gun from the soldier and opened fire on the bomber. One had to be quick on the draw to live in such attacks. As he did so he clearly saw the bombs leave the aircraft.

On the gun-deck all guns were ready for firing. It was just the stupefying surprise of the aircraft's attack which caused the hesitation and the time needed to execute the 'Fire' order. Then a shower of bullets and shells erupted from the dark vessel and tore upward at the bomber. Some of the bullets ripped into the nose and fuselage of the Dornier. But it was not so much the damage they did as the surprise of the ship's reply which was sufficient to affect the airman's aim. Seamen saw the bombs wobble in the air then plunge into the water and explode. Two pillars of white foam, only a few dozen yards from the port side of the steamer, rose almost to mast height. The explosions were so close the ship was rocked and smothered in a deluge of sea-water and the shock waves hit the ship rattling the hull like a tin can. Every man exposed to the cascade wondered just what was happening as the thunder of the bursting bombs mingled with the roar of the Dornier's two engines as she swept on.

At full power the aircraft climbed up and away from the fire-spitting freighter. She circled astern in a wide arc to starboard, the sound of her engines growing fainter as they were throttled back. The gun layer recognised the distinctive sound of the Daimler-Benz engines. The bomber was obviously preparing for her next run-in. But she had now lost the advantage of surprise. The gunners on the ship beneath her would be ready for the next attack. The odds were not altogether in her favour. Nevertheless she had found a straggler and although it would spit and bite, this was the kind of target the airmen preferred.

Clad in duffel-coats and steel-helmeted, the seamen waited, for they knew what was in store for them and the next few minutes could mean death . . . or life. They felt their slow-moving ship was relatively easy meat for the attacker as she plugged on miles behind the convoy. At their speed they could take no effective evasive action and must face the hunter.

Every eye scanned the sky astern where the drone of the bomber's engines came down to them out of the dark, windward sky. Captain Grimstone and the officers on the bridge could give no further orders – the issue lay with the gunners. And it sounded to them as if the bomber was flying low, perhaps a mere 500 feet. She was probably manoeuvring to sweep down again upon them in a shallow dive.

So engrossed were the crew of the steamer in straining eyes and ears to locate the aircraft that they failed to observe the long, grey shape that swept towards them through the choppy seas on their starboard side. But all at once it looked as if someone had lit an immense bonfire on the surface of the sea only a few hundred yards from them – a bonfire that roared and crackled and sent darting tongues of flame reaching into the clouds. At the sound of the bombing, the destroyer *HMS Vesper*, hurling the sea away from her bows like the Severn bore, had raced back from her station astern of the convoy to assist the freighter. Like a sheepdog watching over the flock, she had sped back to help the threatened straggler. She took the crew of the bomber, as well as the crew of the *English Trader* by utter surprise. It must have looked from the air like a Guy Fawkes night party. The Dornier swung sharply away, dropping two more bombs. Both were well wide of their target.

It is certain that the German aircraft received damage, either from the destroyer's barrage or the earlier reply from the *English Trader*. Perhaps it preferred something less lethal to attack for it had received a sharp answer to its questions. It made off into the night and did not resume its attack. The *English Trader* was left with her other problems.

An hour passed with the crew of the steamer talking among themselves of the air attack and the near misses of the first assault. There was no further indication of enemy air activity and the men of both the *English Trader* and *HMS Vesper* were hoping that they would be left alone for the remainder of the night. It was, however, but wishful thinking, for it was unlikely that the Germans, pursuing an intensive campaign with aircraft against coastal shipping, once they had found a valuable convoy moving within easy range – especially as one of them was adrift – would let the hours of darkness pass without a further attempt to damage it.

At half-past eight, the sound of a plane was heard coming from the west. It got nearer and passed almost overhead, but it was flying high and in the dark sky no one actually saw it. Alarm bells were set ringing throughout the steamer, and the sound of shouted orders drifted across the water from the escort as she, too, prepared for further action.

A hundred men on the two waiting ships listened as the engine noise grew stronger. Then a row of parachute flares blossomed out and, hanging below the blanket of clouds, resembled brilliant lanterns with swirling smoke drifting upwards. The burning magnesium lit up the sea over a large area, but the flares were at least a mile away. Gradually the brilliant flares lowered to the sea and the cold waters quenched them. The sharp eyes of the German bomber crew had not been able to detect the two ships below. Although the seamen felt naked, as in the glare of footlights, the dark grey ships on the ever-moving water were not so easily discerned.

There were minutes of anxiety as the flares burned, but even when darkness closed in each seaman listened keenly as the engines of the plane were heard while it made a wide, sweeping detour. Then again, the drone became a roar almost above them. The men on the target ships waited, some literally with bated breath, hoping and praying that the enemy in the darkness above would drop no flares at that moment. They heaved sighs of relief as the Dornier swept farther away from them and when it did light flares again they were more distant. The Germans had been given a fairly precise position of the ships of the convoy and they did not easily give up; the search went on a long time. But the darkness was being a friend to the British vessels, and after what felt to the watching gunners an age, the enemy abandoned the hunt and flew off.

The crews of the freighter and destroyer were left wondering how the Germans had failed to spot them in the light of the first set of flares for the detail of each ship was visible to the other. The gunners could even see the ratings on the destroyer. It was evident that the *English Trader* was fated not to die at the hands of the enemy!

Midnight Saturday 25th October, eight bells, and all was quiet except for the usual sounds of a ship. The propeller was now turning at little more than three-quarters of its normal revolutions. The ship was rolling slightly at about five degrees in a long, shallow swell as she plodded northwards. From the northeast a light breeze was still shaking the rigging.

When it seemed safe to assume that the Germans had given up their search, the gun-watch below (which had been called to the gun-deck), were allowed to return to their quarters on the understanding that they should be prepared to take up action stations at the first sign of further trouble. Fully dressed, each man rolled into his hammock. And about midnight the entire crew were, more or less, on normal watch-keeping. The eight gunners were on watch-and-watch (four hours on watch, four hours off), until the ship reached a less dangerous area.

As one of the relieving four men took over the watch, he called out to those going below: 'Let's hope we don't have to turn you chaps out before four o'clock.' But they were to be turned out – for a different reason to what the well-wisher had thought.

HMS Vesper returned to her station with the convoy.

The crew of the *English Trader* no doubt wondered why the captain maintained his course northward, although lagging so many miles behind the group. They queried: 'Would it not have been wiser to put in to Harwich or Yarmouth?'

There were, however, for Captain Grimstone, other factors to consider – E-boats lurked in the approaches to the harbours. In fact, the channel between the Haisborough Sands and the East Coast was nicknamed by sailors 'E-boat alley'. Possibly, the protection of the destroyer also weighed in the captain's decision to keep course. If he turned and ran for port he would lose that. Undoubtedly, he discussed the matter with his officers and then took what they thought to be the wisest course. But it was really Hobson's Choice. Captain Grimstone was a seasoned and capable master who knew the dangers to be met whatever decision he took, and his action in staying on course was the best, in his judgment.

CHAPTER 3
Aground on Hammond Knoll

 SUNDAY, OCTOBER 26th came and the crew felt on that night – as many a time before – that the hours of the middle watch dragged more than any other. In coastal waters it was usually a quiet watch and, therefore, somewhat more lonely. Naturally, nobody made more noise than was necessary. And when men talked, should the opportunity occur, they spoke in subdued voices. It was like that on this fateful night, at least at the beginning.

The moon was dipping towards the western horizon, its light penetrating the clouds in a murkish almost greenish grey. The watch-keepers could see little beyond the ship. There was no increase in the force of the wind but it was definitely colder and the men were glad of their duffel coats. At intervals, the winking lights of the buoys came into view shining across the inky water, and then they passed and disappeared astern. The ship's speed had made a little favourable increase, but as she shouldered the waves, it could be noticed that a vibration was passing through the decks, probably caused by an adverse tide pushing against the hull.

The convoy was routed to stand well out from Lowestoft and Yarmouth and proceeding west of the Newark light vessel station (removed in wartime), it was steaming through the wide, buoyed channel between the Hammond Knoll to starboard, and the Haisborough Sands to port.

Between 1 am and 1.30 am the vessel was in the grip of a really strong ebb tide and was making little progress against it. She was also dangerously near to the sandbank of Hammond Knoll which lay less than half a mile on the starboard bow. This sandbank was hidden from the sailor's view by 20 feet of water and presented little danger to craft of shallow draught. Before the melting of the ice of the last Ice Age when Britain was joined to the Continent, Hammond Knoll was – as the name suggests – 'a small hill or mound'.

About 1.45 am there was a sudden though slight jolt. It was as if the ship had paused for a moment. Immediately and urgently, the engine-room telegraph rang. But before the engines could be stopped there was a second and more severe jolt.

It flung the gunners who were on their feet across the deck. The deck itself seemed to shoot forward sending the men flying astern. This jolt was followed by a grinding and rending from the bottom of the vessel. The crunching sound ended in a dull rumbling. It stopped and there was a dead silence. A strange silence. For a full minute there was no further sound or movement. The ship had stopped in its tracks. The tide-rip had caught the big ship in its mighty grip and pushed her firmly aground.

Then there came a loud rattle and clatter of chains from the engine-room. This was promptly followed by a hiss of steam and the ship's screw began turning in reverse. She shuddered in her bowels with the strain. The speed of the propeller increased until it shook the entire vessel. The vibration was violent. It filled the ship. The great mass of thousands of tons of steel rattled until it seemed the vessel would crack and come apart. There followed a loud, metallic clang, as if a heavy object had been dropped from a considerable height into the engine-room. The terrific, frightening shaking ceased abruptly as the engine stopped. Then came the noise of steam escaping under high pressure. There was a shout, urgent and alarmed. The hiss of steam grew in intensity until it was deafening. It lasted a couple of painful minutes, then a man's scream of pain pierced the hissing of steam until, somewhere below, a valve was closed and the tumult dropped gradually until it became but a whisper and then faded completely. All was again silent, but somewhere down there in the boiler-room a man had been scalded to death.

Just what happened in the engine-room is not known, but Fireman A J Pugh died in the accident and two other firemen were injured. It is possible that the engine-room was flooded, if not wholly then in part, for the body of Fireman Pugh could not be got out. The other two men were assisted on deck and helped forward.

For what seemed a very long time the gunners heard no sound in the ship other than the wind sighing through the wires and the sea slapping against the barnacled hull. Then someone was heard running along the starboard alleyway. Voices drifted up to them: voices in urgent conversation. Once more the sound of hurrying footsteps along the deck and again that strange silence, ominous and uncanny – just as though there was no other life nor movement in the vessel. It still remains in William Hickson's mind as something so unreal and eerie as though the grounding of his vessel had turned it into a ghost ship.

A quarter of an hour passed – a period of apprehension and bewilderment. It was one of the oddest fifteen minutes the gun layer had ever known. The after-end of the ship had become most lonely. Where were the other 45 men? What were they doing? Why was everything so deathly still?

All around was the unfriendly darkness of the North Sea; the sound of waves washing the ship's sides; the wind complaining overhead and the black outline of the freighter. But there was no sound of men calling for assistance. No conversation or shouted orders. No clumping of seaboots on the deck. It engendered an oppressive sense of desertion. One of the gunners broke their thoughts: 'I reckon we're the only ones left back here.'

But they were not. Oddly, the rest of the gunners who were on watch below, had not appeared, so the gun layer decided he ought to go down and see what had happened to them. 'I'll see what's become of them,' he said and descended the ladder from the gun-deck.

He was most surprised to find his men still in their hammocks. Some of them were asleep. He was even more amazed to find that they knew nothing of what had happened to their ship. The ground, the vibration of the engines when unable to move the vessel, the escape of steam, had not roused them.

'We've run onto a sandbank,' William Hickson told the alarmed men as they scrambled hastily out of their hammocks on to the wet deck.

The light in their sleeping quarters was still on. This was a clear proof that the generator was still running. Yet that was odd, for the generator itself was 20 feet or more below the deck on which level the gunners' quarters were built. And it was unlikely because water was already flooding over the deck an inch or so deep. The generator should have been well under water and out of order.

The gun layer knew the ship and its wiring system well for he had helped, on a previous voyage, with some of the wiring problems although it was not his job and he was not a trained electrician. There was no emergency lighting at that level, and now, some 38 years later, the only explanation that William Hickson can advance is that the engine-room was stuck so fast in the sand that the water was unable to enter and the dynamo for that particular part of the ship was still out of the water and running. He remembers that at that period of crisis it made him feel very uneasy, and he was glad to get his men hurriedly from their quarters and sent amidships.

He returned to the gun-deck and told his gunners of his fears, and explained why he was so concerned. It was clear the *English Trader* had run onto the bank because her flagging engine had been unable to cope with the strong push of the ebb tide and she had been shoved, slowly but remorselessly onto the Knoll.

Hammond Knoll lies south-east of the far more dangerous Haisborough Sands which stretch some nine miles long and a mile wide, off the Norfolk coast. They have swallowed more shipping than the notorious Goodwin Sands off Kent. The usual maximum depth of water on the Haisboroughs is 12 feet, but in places is only two feet! Lifeboatmen have walked on them once or twice at low tide. This variation has made these shallows a veritable graveyard of shipping down the centuries and only a few weeks earlier, six ships in one convoy had gone aground on them and broken their backs.

William Hickson believed that the ship had stuck fast along most of her 374 feet length. It proved later that she broke her back for'ard of the bridge due to the scouring action of the seas.

This was not the first time the *English Trader* had been stranded, for as far back as 23rd January 1937, when she was but three years old, she had run aground when entering Dartmouth harbour. She was stranded close to the castle and would not budge despite the efforts of a destroyer and four tugs to get her off the rocks. Ten days later her bows had been so badly holed and some holds filled with debris that it was decided to do a bit of 'ship surgery'. This entailed cutting her in two, and it took nineteen days to do so. The bow section was removed and later cut up for scrap, while the undamaged after part was pulled stern-first into Dartmouth to get the shelter of the river, and later to Southampton. The Middle Docks and Engineering Company of South Shields won the contract for a complete repair which meant rebuilding the *English Trader* from the boiler-room forward. This big job was done in 100 days and the ship was then ready for sea. The size of the job and the credit for its completion in that time is realised when one thinks that 6,000 bags of cement in No 2 hold had first to be taken out by chipping into small pieces.

One wonders if her pronounced roll, making her an uncomfortable ship at times, was due to this remarkable bit of grafting!

Now aground for the second time, on a sandbank, on her gun-deck three men listened with apprehension for any noise that would tell them just what was going on aboard, but they could neither see nor hear anyone on the decks. They expected a telephone call from the bridge with instructions about abandoning the gun-deck but it did not come and the 'phone was obviously out of order.

After what seemed an extremely long-drawn-out time, William Hickson, with seaman-gunner Daniels and a lance-corporal, climbed down from the poop-deck and made their uncertain way, cautiously groping along the inky alleyway leading to the sailors' and firemen's quarters. They called out: 'Is there anyone about?'

There was no reply. They went on to the bo'sun's cabin and banged on his door. Again they shouted.

No answer came. So they opened the door and turned the light switch. There was no light. One of them, Dan, went into the cabin and immediately fell over a bucket. It clattered away into a corner of the room and he swore heartily. Here the water was ankle-deep, sloshing about as they or the ship moved.

Gunner Hickson then felt the after part of the *English Trader* move in an alarming way. The deck heaved up beneath their feet and settled again. He heard the sound of water in the crews' quarters surge and gurgle as it swilled from side to side following the movement of the deck. There was no time nor desire for a committee meeting, but if there had been, the unanimous decision would have been to get out quickly. The three men all made their way for'ard expecting to find the rest of the crew.

They found that the seamen, or most of them, had gathered on the bunker-deck just below the bridge and for'ard of the funnel. They were talking quietly among themselves. No one was sure just what had happened other than that they were stuck firm on a bank. Nor did they know what they were supposed to do. A seaman has fire drill, anti-aircraft drill, lifeboat drill, but he does not rehearse for grounding! They just waited for instructions from their officers, or developments.

Some of the gunners were still keeping watch on the boat-deck with the Oerlikons on their platforms. It was a comparatively safe place for them, at least for the time being. William Hickson went to them and told them to stay there until they had an order to leave.

Captain Grimstone, standing with his officers on the lower bridge, felt they should wait for daylight before making any decision about abandoning ship. It was evident that, like everyone else, he did not know the extent of the damage. He was quite adamant that there was no question of faulty navigation or that the *English Trader* had been driven onto the sandbank because of damage sustained by the enemy bombing. There had been no such damage. She had been grounded by the strong tide and the fact that her flagging engine had not been turning fast enough to counteract the inexorable push of the tide.

Then there came a gust of wind which rattled the halyards and loose rope-ends. It scurried some unseen litter across the decks – like dry leaves on a rural road in autumn at dead of night. The wind stayed and played with the rigging for a few minutes and then was gone.

William Hickson reported to the captain what he had seen in the after part of the vessel. The captain was not surprised. The second mate asked, however, if everyone was clear of that end of the ship. The gunner told him he felt sure they were and the officer asked him why he had not telephoned the bridge before as they were a little worried by his silence, especially as they were unable then to contact the gun-deck from the bridge. This explained why the gunners aft had received no instructions from the captain.

The third mate added: 'We were just thinking about coming to look for you.'

At this moment, even as the captain was speaking to an officer, there came another gust of wind lasting but a few seconds. It whistled through the open spaces between the bridge and the boat-deck. It beat down smoke still coming from the funnel. The master went on to reassure his men that, for the moment, there was nothing to worry about. It seemed to William Hickson that he had not noticed the gusts, and he thought perhaps the captain, being a deep-sea sailor, paid no heed to them, forgetting with his many other concerns, that they could be a warning. But after a minute or so of silence, Captain Grimstone turned to his first mate and quietly said: 'Wind! That's just the last thing we want now.'

The captain called the gunner to him and asked if all the men in the galley had come up. As William Hickson was not sure, he was sent to check for he knew the layout of the ship even in the darkness perhaps better than anyone. So Hickson went to the galley almost amidships. He found five of the crew sitting round the fire. It was much warmer there than on deck but when he told them the captain wished them to come up, they made no demur but left the cosiness of the big fire for the chill night on the open deck and made their way, following Hickson, to join the rest of the ship's company near the lower bridge.

The gusts of wind became more frequent, at times combining to a steady moan which gradually stepped up into a whine. Spray was now being whipped up and flying unseen out of the dark, it hit a man across the face and hands like a whip-lash. The moon set at about 2 am that Sunday morning and as the darkness increased it was as though someone slowly closed a massive door on a windowless room. It was a darkness that could almost be felt.

Perhaps an hour later the wind was blowing steadily. Halyards and rigging were moaning, creaking and shaking. And when the tardy dawn came on that autumn day it showed white breakers moving across the sandbank. They looked very much like bundles of feathers dancing on the surface. One or two miniature 'seahorses' scurried along, glittering white against the dark background of the waves.

Over on the port side of the freighter, the grey silhouette of a ship could be seen. It was recognised as the destroyer *HMS Vesper*. Unbeknown to the crew of the *English Trader*, the escort had taken up a position clear of the sandbank. She stationed herself in the deep water to keep watch over the distressed steamer and also to afford protection should an enemy attack her.

As the tide started to flow, the sea began to lift aboard the vessel. The captain therefore, ordered all the men to move for'ard and some ascended the ladder to the lower bridge.

It was not long before the wind had built up the sea into long racing 'sea horses', with their white, curling crests. Standing on the shore on a windy day they appear as distinct, fast-moving waves with foaming white heads – hell-bent on getting nowhere in particular. They make a spectacular display and are a joy to watch as they bound and leap throwing the spindrift high like the flying mane of a wild horse. On a stranded ship in wartime in the grey light of early day, they give the hungry cold seamen no joy at all.

Through the semi-darkness William Hickson had seen these 'seahorses' here and there. At first they were of no great size. Only their tops swept across the decks of the freighter. There was no great force of wind behind them, but it was increasing with the coming of daylight. This was the time for the seamen on the stranded vessel to take that little extra precaution when moving from place to place even on the lower bridge.

Officers and men now prepared for a long vigil on the stricken ship waiting for daylight to reveal the extent of the damage. Many of the men were ill-clad for the ordeal ahead, but they could do nothing to get warmer clothes for fear of losing touch with their shipmates. Most had only been on board some 30 hours and were unfamiliar with the ship – it might court disaster to go wandering off. They shivered in the cold air as they stood in the lee of the funnel, the boat-deck and the fiddley.

With the hindsight of many years, William Hickson admits that he made two mistakes at this time, mistakes which he should have avoided had he given more thought to what he was doing – mistakes that almost cost him his life. For some reason the ship's electrical alarm system developed a fault which set all the alarm bells ringing throughout the vessel. Captain Grimstone was standing against the bulkhead of the wireless room. With all the worries on his mind, the loud clanging of the bells grated on him. He endured the din for a time then asked the gunner if he could do something about it because the noise was getting on his nerves. Again the job fell to William Hickson for his knowledge of the *English Trader* and her wiring system.

'Right, sir,' said the gunner and went off with the wind tugging at this clothes, to see if he could silence the clamour. The light was slowly increasing and he found no difficulty in getting about the ship.

Most of the bells were easy to get at and it was just a matter of seconds to put them out of action by twisting the hammer away from the contacts. He quickly silenced the one in the engineers' alleyway and the officers' part of the ship. He saw that the vessel's engines were totally submerged. He dealt with all the bells – that is all but one, and that was just outside his own cabin in the alleyway aft, next door to the bo'sun's cabin. It was almost at the end of the ship.

He has since reflected that it is unlikely this bell, so far aft could be heard by the captain from the bridge, and he might well have left it sounding its wild warning over the sea without worrying anyone. The noise of wind and swirling water would probably have drowned its ringing. Nevertheless, he decided to finish his job and put it out of action. So he crossed the short well-deck and climbed the ladder to the poop. He entered the alley by the portside door and locating the bell by its clanging, twisted the hammer and silenced it.

He had done what he was told to do and if he had retraced his footsteps at once, he could have done so quite safely. But being near his own cabin he thought he would go inside – just to have a last look at the little room where he had spent so much of his time for the 22 months since he joined the *English Trader*.

Inside the cabin which he had carefully decorated soon after joining the ship – and causing the captain to remark: 'Your cabin is smarter than mine, Gunner!' – he found the dead-lights were clamped down over the porthole making the room totally dark. William Hickson went to the starboard port and unscrewed the deadlight. He then stood for several minutes looking out over the sandbank watching the seahorses rolling towards his ship in the pale light of the early autumn day. They were some distance away and did not seem to be running in a direct line, but from his low-level viewpoint they appeared big and powerful.

He sat down on a small settee in the gloom of the cabin and looked about him. He noticed his seaboots standing by his bunk. He bent forward to pick them up with the intention of taking them back with him to the bridge. As he did so a giant wave hit the vessel with tremendous force. The cabin was plunged into utter darkness as the mass of green water surged over the porthole totally obscuring the light. There was a great roar overhead as tons of water thundered over the gun-deck above him. The deck beneath him lifted and tilted sideways, and then dropped again as the surge of water passed under the stern. From somewhere deep down in the freighter, a hollow boom echoed up to him. It was an alarming experience. It demonstrated the might of the sea and his own helplessness against such terrific forces. Seaman that he was, he had never felt it so strongly before.

For a moment William Hickson did not know what he should do. Nor did he know just what had happened. It flashed across his mind how very foolish he had been to tarry in his cabin; and even more thoughtless not to have told someone just where he was going. He was quite alone, right in the stern of the ship and no one would know where to look for him. He had been a sailor long enough to be more sea-wary, and he muttered almost angrily to himself: 'Hickson, it's time to get out – quickly!'

With his seaboots beneath his arm he rushed out of his cabin and along the alleyway to the open deck intending to make a dash for the main deck. But he stopped in his tracks. He saw immediately that during the short time he had been aft putting the bell out of action, reflecting in his cabin and gazing at the seahorses, the mood of the sea had worsened appreciably. In a matter of ten to fifteen minutes the waves had so increased that he was now in real peril of being caught by one of the combers which were rolling across the well-deck, some indeed nearly reaching as high as the poop. William Hickson knew he must try to reach the shelter of the mainmast and winches but this meant going down one ladder, across the well-deck and up another ladder before he could get between the mast and the winches, taking the shelter they afforded. Although all ladders to the bridge were of the stairway type with handrails, those to the boat-deck were runged horizontally and had to be climbed. This was far less easy.

It was at this time he gave heartfelt thanks to the bo'sun who had prepared the fog marker-buoy on the previous morning – so many action-filled hours before. The bo'sun had carried the line from the mast to be ready for throwing the buoy astern should fog come down quickly – a usual precaution in convoys – and the line was now like a lifeline for Hickson. It stretched along the bulkhead just above the door where he was standing. He reach up and gripped it. Clinging to the rope, he stood for a minute or so trying to sum up the situation. Then he moved forward endeavouring to see across to the weather-side where the waves were sweeping onto the steamer. But the superstructure blocked his view. He could not safely get far enough out to see them. He dared not chance making a dash without knowing how close was the next big sea and the uproar of wind and rushing water about him did not permit him to rely on his hearing. To make a blind rush would have been suicidal as there seemed to be hardly any time between each successive wave.

The change in the temper of the sea during the brief time since he had last crossed this same deck was unbelievable even to him, a seaman for many years.

He threw his seaboots away and watched them float off through the ship's rails. As he did so a towering wave hit the *English Trader* half burying him in its green bulk. With his back pressed hard against the steel bulkhead and gripping the line over his head with all his strength, he somehow held on. The bulkhead shielded him from much of the force of the water, otherwise it would just have wrenched him from his hold like a rag doll and tossed him where it chose. The strongest man's grip is broken by such forces.

The length of time that William Hickson stood there not knowing what to do but sure that a false move might be his death, and feeling sick at heart at his own folly, could probably be counted in minutes, but as he held tightly on, waist-deep in the swirling icy water and drenched from head to foot, it seemed a very, very long time. They were the worst moments of his sea-going career.

Then came a lull, just a matter of moments, but long enough for him to wonder if he dare make the dash down the ladder and across the deck. Even so, he was still unable to see how close the next wave was running. He just dared not take the risk. So he clung there fearful and bewildered.

The predicament was worse because the seas were running in any direction, being pushed out of deep water by the strong wind and also by the tide. In the open sea an experienced sailor knows roughly the space between each wave. He can judge the length of time he has got to cross a given space, but that was not so here on Hammond Knoll in this storm. The waves came in from any quarter, some treading on each other's heels. Others were well spaced out. They were huge – green monsters, with teeth. He heard their deep-throated baying as they raced over the sandbank like a pack of hounds. William Hickson knew he could climb up to the gun-deck above him – but he would then be even more exposed and marooned, and it meant putting more obstacles between him and the bridge where his shipmates were.

Then, with a relief such as he had never known before, he saw through the scurry of flying spray, a figure coming towards him along the main deck. The man had his head down against the gale, and he swayed and dodged between the ventilators and the hatch, seeking any shelter he could get. As the figure got closer William Hickson recognised Seaman-Gunner Daniels – Dan.

Worried about the long absence of the gun layer, Dan had come to look for him. William Hickson waited anxiously until his gunner had reached the winch nearest to him, close to the ladder which he must climb. The well-deck was the gap between them. Dan crouched down, using the winch for protection but gazing at the sea on the weather-side. He raised his hand high in the air and waited. William Hickson knew that when the arm dropped he must make a dash literally for his life across that short intervening space. Two waves came snorting over the well-deck. There was a brief lull and the gun layer saw Dan's arm drop and heard him yell:'Now!'

He made the crucial dash, down the ladder, across the well-deck and up the other ladder faster than he had ever before moved in all his years. But he reached the shelter of the winches with Dan grabbing an arm to help him at the top of the ladder. Even as he did so, with Dan's hand still clutching his duffel coat, a sea came aboard and broke over both men. The winches however, took the full force of the rushing water, thus protecting them as they clung on with desperation to any hand-hold.

The two gunners then hurried back, dodging round anything that offered a lee, to the lower bridge. They reached it, breathless and drenched, with William Hickson very shaken. The gun layer's duffel coat was so full of water he took it off and threw it away. His socks too ran with water, but he dare not discard them. He just kept his trousers, shirt and a light naval jacket which he wore under his duffel coat. It was little enough protection for the grim hours ahead.

The clock moved round to 7.30 am. The wind had reached full gale force. The seahorses were bigger, more powerful and more menacing. They were galloping across the decks of the ship fore and aft. Soon, William Hickson knew, they would change shape as they grew even bigger and become giant 'greenbacks' which tower high and run before the wind like long, grey-green hills.

In the light of day, Captain Grimstone was able to assess the plight of his ship. She was doomed. There was no hope of refloating or towing her free and practically no hope of getting his men away in their own lifeboats. Long before, he had instructed his radio operator, Sparks, to send a distress signal. This went out at dawn when it was plain that, with the weather rapidly worsening, the only lifeboat in the *English Trader* which could be used would be on the port or lee side, and neither officers nor men were optimistic that this could be launched successfully, much less clear the turbulent seas running on the sandbank.

By 8 am when it was broad daylight, the sea had built up to such an extent that it would have courted disaster even to attempt to get this boat away. What help there was for the men must now come from outside the vessel.

Throughout the night the destroyer had stood watch over her unhappy charge. She received a message from the shore to the effect that the *English Trader's* call for help had been heard and that immediate rescue operations were being organised. Sparks still kept his listening post and confirmed that the message was correct. No one yet knew from what source help would come.

CHAPTER 4
Three Men Swept Overboard

 ABOUT 9 am on Sunday October 26th there came the first sign that rescue operations were well in hand. A small Lysander aircraft, battling against the NNE gale signalled with a lamp: 'Hold on! Help is coming! Good luck!'

At the same moment as the low-flying plane passed directly over the freighter, the bo'sun and Able Seaman Joseph Biss noticed that the port lifeboat, which was the only one which could be used if the chance came, had broken loose in its davits and was swinging to and fro. The starboard boat had already been smashed by the sea. The two men agreed that they ought to make it secure in case it was required. On what small decisions hang the issues of life and death! That quickly-taken resolve was to bring a dire result.

So far, the heavy seas had not reached the boat-deck although hard, wind-driven spray was flying continuously over it and both men realised that it would be no easy job to make the boat fast. Nevertheless, they were determined to try.

Buffeted by the storm and lashed by the spray, the bo'sun led the way. They managed to reach the boat-deck where, for some ten minutes, they were busy tightening and securing ropes and lashing the boat fast in its chocks. Then having completed their task, they turned to come back to the lower bridge, and had nearly reached the top of the ladder leading down to the the bunker-deck. As they did so there came an urgent warning from several mariners on the bridge who had been watching them. Both men swung round and saw, to their dismay, a great wave rolling over the starboard side of the ship towards them. They turned and ran, trying desperately to reach a funnel stay. But the wall of water was upon them. The bo'sun was in time to grab the stay and brace himself. The onrush of water however, caught Joe Biss before he could get a handhold on the stay. The wave just picked him up and swept him clear over the rails and out of the ship.

Most of the crew were on the lower bridge and the others above them on the navigation bridge. They stood horrified as they saw their shipmate snatched up and borne on the crest of that deadly wave. There was no help they could give. No thrown lifebuoy or coil of rope would have reached him. They had shouted their warning but it was too late. Now they could only cry out in dismay.

The airmen in the Lysander which was still circling the *English Trader*, saw the accident and immediately dived their small manoeuvrable plane down to within a few dozen feet of the seaman who lay on his back, halfway between the trough and the crest of the wave. They dropped almost at once, a yellow, inflated raft or float. It hit the sea close to the desperate man but even as he struggled to grasp it, the strong wind caught it and snatched the float beyond his grasp.

The watchers saw Joe roll over on his side on the crest of the following wave, facing the ship and, raising his arm high they faintly heard his oft-repeated catch phrase: 'Taxi! Taxi!' as he was carried away. Joe was saying farewell to his mates in the way he had so often greeted them as they passed one another on the decks.

Joe Biss had a wife and three children. He was known among his comrades as Happy Joe, for he was always ready with a wisecrack or joke. Even in the grimmest situation he saw the brighter side. His phrase when hailing another seaman on the ship was: 'Taxi! Taxi!' His death struck the entire crew like a body punch for they had seen how, in a flash, when the *English Trader* 'took it green', these powerful seas could claim a victim. This time the man they had taken could ill be spared in this crisis, for his good spirits in times of boredom and when tempers were roused, were both a tonic and a sedative to his shipmates. Those gifts would have been priceless in the ordeal now awaiting the stranded crew.

The bo'sun got back safely, ashen-faced and shocked. He had been almost by Joe's side when the sea took him. He knew how close he also had been to a similar death. A split second of time – a matter of two or three feet – had saved him. But for his desperate grip on the stay he must have been pulled off the ship.

That wave which seized Joe Biss was the first grim warning that the seahorses had taken on their new and even more formidable shape and size, of greenbacks. It was the first sea surge over the boat-deck. Soon however, it was followed by other massive waves that rode high, majestic and threatening. Swift and silent, they moved like hills showing nearly all sea, just a small curling white top until they hit the *English Trader* with a thunderous roar, passed over it showing their long, sloping backs. They slid onwards to port, leaving a frothing foam on the decks.

The Lysander crew saw what was happening but knew there was nothing more they could do, and they were endangering themselves by staying in the area with the wind at its present blustering strength. It was also likely that they had to report back to their base. No one was surprised therefore, to see them signal the destroyer that they were returning, and turn landwards.

At the very time that Joe Biss and the bo'sun were working on the lifeboat, Chief Engineer A Berry made up his mind suddenly that it was an opportune moment for him to go to his cabin which was under the boat-deck, and change out of overalls into his best uniform. He turned to another officer, saying: 'I can't go ashore in these dirty overalls when the lifeboat comes. I'll just go and change into my best clothes.'

Again a minor decision – but what a major consequence!

He left the lower bridge and walked along the deck to his cabin in the after end of the deck-houses. He was gone for at least a quarter of an hour and it was only by the merest chance that someone spotted him coming back from his cabin. He could have been in dire danger from the very moment that he came out again from that door. He had just got past the funnel and had reached the door of the fiddley – the entrance to the stoke-hole. Then he continued to cross the open space by the bunker-hatch (a distance of little more than 15 feet) to reach the bridge ladder. John Elliott saw him and shouted, warning him of a towering wave advancing on the *English Trader*. Possibly he did not hear the shout above the tumult of churning water and the wind's screaming. He had not known of course, what had happened to Joe Biss, otherwise he would have been more aware of his own danger in crossing the bunker-deck. No one will know, for he continued walking without even looking to see if it was safe to do so.

The sea hit the ship with a mighty roar and poured over the bunker-hatch at least ten feet deep. It broke in a fury of foam and swirling water. A lot of it actually surged right over the lower bridge where many of the men were standing. Too late the chief engineer saw it. He made as if to dash forward then put up his arms as if to ward off the onrush of brine. But the wave caught him and picked him up hurling him against a steel stanchion. Then it flung him back again as it poured onwards. to leave him lying on the deck seriously injured.

The cook, R Thomas, who was standing at the top of the lower-bridge ladder, seeing the prostrate man below, hurried down to get him. He too, in his anxiety, failed to see the danger that was already racing towards him, for the following wave was almost on the heels of the giant which had smashed the engineer.

The third mate, John Elliott, yelled to William Hickson: 'Gunner, cut the signal halyard!'

The gun layer always carried a knife and in a flash he cut through the new signal halyard, drawing it out of its pulley and whipping it around John Elliott's waist. The other end was thrown upwards and grasped by several seamen on the deck above. The third mate was halfway down the ladder, hurrying to assist the cook when the wave stuck the vessel. It roared like an express train crashing through a station, across the gap between bridge and funnel. The cook had almost reached the prostrate bleeding engineer when the oncoming sea grabbed him. It lifted him right off his feet as if he was but a straw and washed him under the overhanging canopy of the bridge.

John Elliott clung to the ladder, pressing himself against it as the water thundered over him, then swept on. Recovering his breath he went further down the ladder, but the shouts from his shipmates above him and the tugging of the rope around him made him attend to his own safety. Already, another immense sea hurrying on the steps of the last, was sweeping towards them. It could as easily treat him, rope or no rope, as it had the chief engineer.

The wave was on them. It appeared to tower above the steamer, big as it was, then hit the *English Trader* amidships, rolling *en masse* right over the boat-deck. Sliding around the funnel and swirling to the bunker-deck, it careered in a hissing, snarling mass about the top of the bridge ladder.

When it passed off the ship, the cook and the chief engineer had gone! Both were swept overboard into the sea boiling in anger about the freighter. No one, other than John Elliott, saw them go, so deep was the water of that murdering sea.

John Elliott climbed hurriedly back up the ladder, drenched and shaken. Water poured out of his clothes as he turned and looked back to see the empty swilling deck and knew that his brave effort was really hopeless. The sea was supreme here.

Three men had been carried overboard within a few minutes. Captain Grimstone immediately gave the order that no man was to leave the bridge decks without his express permission. The seriousness of their situation was clear to all – rescue was far from a certainty. The grave looks of the rest of the crew said more than words what they were feeling at this additional tragedy.

John Elliott gasped to William Hickson as he undid the rope about him: 'The old cook was still alive, but like the engineer, he was smashed to pieces. I saw him go over the side.'

Much earlier, the steward, who had made many voyages in the *English Trader,* had summed up the situation of his ship long before the storm gained major proportions. He had gone to his pantry below the bridge and collected all the cigarettes he could carry. Unfortunately, he was unable to get food or drink as they were all under water, but as he carried the tins of cigarettes up the ladder and into the chartroom, he remarked: 'There's no telling how much longer we shall be here, so I see no reason why we should go short of a smoke!'

By the number of tins of State Express 333 he – and later one of the gunners – carried from the pantry, it looked as if he expected the stay to be a long one. When someone made a remark to this effect, he simply laughed and said: 'Better too many than not enough and they'd be no good if they were left down there.'

The tins were handed round. William Hickson still keeps one of his tins in his joiner's workshop. At the moment it is used to hold odd screws and nails, but it also holds memories of that wild night on Hammond Knoll.

At first, on that Sunday morning, no one had doubted that their rescue was just a matter of waiting a few hours. Few mariners gave much thought to the manner in which this would be carried out. The distress signals had been acknowledged by the Lysander, so it would be but a question of time before help arrived.

However, with the triple tragedy and the North Sea showing a ferocity they had not imagined, the greenbacks hurling themselves at and over their ship, smashing parts of it as though they were made of balsa wood, they began to ask questions. It was not now a sure thing that a lifeboat could get them off the ship, for what boat could live with these wild seas sweeping in from various angles. *HMS Vesper* knew they could not get near them and she had no small boat able to get through waves on the bank. Such rescues were not the role of destroyers.

Still, they had been assured that help was on its way from the Norfolk shore. There was no option open but to resign themselves to wait, making themselves as comfortable as the conditions allowed.

By the middle of that Sunday morning when westward of them in small villages and towns like Sheringham and Cromer, services were being held in church and chapel and prayers were being offered for 'those in peril on the sea,' the men stood on the open lower bridge, wet, cold and wondering how long before that promised help would come. Meanwhile they saw the hungry North Sea tear the ship apart just as a fierce animal tears its victim. Mostly the men were silent for the uproar of the elements made speech difficult.

All four cargo hatches had long since been stove in, and as far as the eye could reach the sea to the westward was littered with small and large boxes as the cargo was dragged from the broached holds. The bold slogans were there: BRITAIN DELIVERS THE GOODS, but these things were not to be unloaded by dark-skinned shore gangs in Mombasa as intended. They were being looted by rapacious seas and tossed about, thousands of pounds worth of merchandise bobbing and tumbling until at last they sank.

Meanwhile they offered a grave risk to any lifeboat which might try to thread a way through them to the *English Trader*. Even as the men watched this plundering, a red-painted tractor was seized from No 1 hold and thrown up onto the deck. Then it was rolled, not on its wheels but bodily sideways until it crashed through the ship's rails leaving a jagged twisted gap.

The seamen did not think it possible for the sea to increase in fury, but now at noon it did so, for the rising tide was adding to the mass and confusion of waters on the Knoll. Waves were hitting the ship as if trying to bulldoze it out of their path. The ship's lifeboat, that the bo'sun and Joe Biss had risked their lives to secure, had been wrenched from its davits and washed away. The davits, with frayed ropes dangling from them, swung to and fro. The ship now had only its rafts left, one in the bows and the other near the mainmast. Both were impossible to reach.

One of the older sailors ventured to approach Captain Grimstone and ask how long he thought the lifeboats would be in reaching them. The captain shook his head. 'They've a long way to come,' he said. 'Over 20 miles against the tide and this sea. It will take them four or five hours' journey. But don't you worry, lads, they will get here, make no mistake about that.'

At about 11 am, five men standing in a group, were looking at the ship rising and falling and wondering just how long it would be before she broke into two parts. As they watched, one of them sighted a small black object bobbing about in the water a hundred yards away almost under the ship's stern. It was difficult to be sure what it was for very little of it showed above the water and it was frequently lost from view entirely as the churning seas cascaded from off the ship's decks over it. It seemed to be held fast by a length of rope or steel cable to the *English Trader's* propeller, or possibly her rudder. It was never more than eight to ten feet from the ship.

Perhaps, because the men were deep-sea sailors, they did not immediately identify this dome-shaped object for what it was – a mine. Possibly, in their present plight, they had forgotten the other enemy.

Suddenly the object lifted. Its cable lengthened as it swung round towards the hull, below the well-deck. The watching men shouted a warning and moved as far as they could get from the object, and the expected explosion. But they still kept their eyes on the bobbing mine as its horns slowly revolved around its perimeter. It was very close to the ship. Twice the mine slewed round and each time its cable lengthened bringing it nearer midships where it was least welcome. Somewhere below No 3 hatch seemed where it might strike the ship.

Then the unwelcome visitor was caught up by a wave that surged round the stern of the freighter and pushed it a dozen or fifteen feet away from the hull. Its cable was now free allowing it to float unobstructed until it passed astern of the destroyer. On *HMS Vesper,* a couple of rifle marksmen spent some minutes drilling holes in the round steel body. Thankfully, it sank.

It may have been British but it was more likely German, for enemy aircraft sowed a few mines overnight and nipped home before daylight.

Noon came and went with the wind shrieking and the booming seas making an unceasing uproar. Steel hatch-covers, broken timbers and ropes littered the decks. Crates of all sizes, part of the cargo, were riding wave crests like jockeys. Some, after being snatched off the ship, were caught by a conflicting wave and flung back on board as though unwanted. As far as a man could see, tens of thousands of pounds worth of merchandise strewed the water. The whisky, the Andrews Liver Salts, the dresses and goodness knows what else, were the sport of the waves.

The *English Trader* was no longer a ship but a wreck. Only a man who has lived through such a situation can conceive what the sea can do when its anger is roused and it has clawed its victim down. Wood, iron and steel would not stay joined together against such hammering. Rivets and welding were no longer a bond. The crew were down to 44 men. Cold and brine-soaked they grouped themselves as far from the spray as they could but with salt water still running from hair and down their faces. They were miserably helpless. Their eyes were bleary with the force of the wind and the salt spray as they watched the hazy western horizon for the first glimpse of a small boat that, despite its puny size in these big seas, was their hope of rescue.

Lifeboats have evolved since 1786 for the very purpose of getting through tumbling surf on a beach and confused waters on banks. Almost two hundred years of hard-won experience and experiment had been built into the boat they hoped would soon be seen.*   *See Note 2, p 95*

The seamen expressed no impatience as their long wait grew longer and longer. Standing in the lee of the bridge-housing, sorting themselves out into their own little groups of shipmates, they lit the cigarettes given them by the steward and watched the blue smoke whipped away by the gale. Many of the men had already taken refuge in the chartroom for it was less cold and the spray and wind could not get at them. It was also easier to talk as one did not have to shout down the wind's abuse and the sea's threats. Additionally, it was possible to rest one's body by sitting on the table-top or an upturned bucket.

Sunday dinnertime came, but of course, no dinner. And at one o'clock the *Vesper* signalled the long-awaited news: 'Lifeboat in sight!'

The second mate called down from the bridge: 'The destroyer says she has sighted a lifeboat.' It was indeed good news and it is a phrase that has brought hope and comfort to countless men around our storm-beset shores.

Now, the seamen were even more anxious to sight the approaching craft although they were not sure in what part of that troubled sea they could expect to see her. Shielding their eyes against the stinging wind by cupping their hands, they searched the far grey and white waters for the tiny flicker of a bow wave. That would be their first sight of a lifeboat.

Some minutes went by and no sighting was obtained. So long had they to wait that they began to wonder if the destroyer had given a mistaken message. Then a sharp-sighted man cried: 'There she is!'

He pointed with eager outstretched arm towards a point astern of the destroyer Then they all picked out a small plume of white spray feathered up, suspended for a moment, and drifted away with the wind. It was followed by another in the same place. The little wisp of spray told of a boat battling towards them through heavy seas. They lost sight of it, then perhaps a couple of minutes later, a degree or so to starboard, they saw it again – a white feather of water leap high and drift to leeward. It died down. It was there again. The sailors, mostly keen-eyed, strained their sight to catch a glimpse of the boat itself. Each man had his own thoughts and his own questions.

They were not to know that at that moment, the boat marked by the drift of spray, getting closer each minute, was one of the best in the fleet and manned by a top-notch crew, all longshore fishermen who knew how to handle a boat and to respect the sea. It was also one of the busiest boats in the Service, for here on the East Coast throughout the war, the lifeboats were in heavy demand. If it was not trouble brought on by the sea it was the activities of the enemy on the surface, under the surface and in the air. Contact, magnetic, acoustic mines, torpedoes, bombs and machine-gun fire were some of the man-made evils that kept the lifeboats in demand, for this East Coast was far too close to Occupied Europe for comfort. Only at the mouth of the Humber was the lifeboat in greater demand than along this stretch of Norfolk coast.

Stubble-chinned and bedraggled, at last the seamen made out the blue and white paintwork of the lifeboat and gradually she took definite shape, although pitching and tossing as she bowed the waves. Oilskin-clad figures could be discerned on deck for a moment, then a curtain of spindrift hid them.

So engrossed were the seamen who had remained on the lower bridge to watch that they were negligent of their own safety and did not see or apparently hear, an oncoming monster wave that rolled at an oblique angle across the boat-deck. A lusty yell from the navigating bridge roused them and sent them scuttling for safety up the ladder. They were only just in time to avoid another thorough dousing, if nothing worse, for the wave sliced, several feet deep, across the deck upon which they had been standing. As it was the last ones only got the water round their legs and a shower of salt water down the backs of their necks.

The crew were not all on the navigating bridge. Some were in the chartroom, others stood outside it. No one ventured into the wheelhouse for it was dark and forbidding on account of the steel shutters that covered the windows, and the starboard door had been damaged, letting in the cold wind and plenty of water. Moreoever, the starboard wing of the bridge was in a most dangerous state. It looked as if it might collapse at any time. Fortunately for their peace of mind, most of the men did not know this. Those that had observed it, kept it discreetly to themselves but wondered what might happen if a curling breaker hit it fair and square.

CHAPTER 5
'Lifeboat on the Way'

EARLIER, ON the Norfolk coast, men had been stirred to swift action when, as the eight o'clock news was being broadcast on that Sunday morning, the Cromer coastguard called Coxswain Henry Blogg on the telephone at his home in Swallow Cottage, and told him the Yarmouth Naval base had asked for a lifeboat to go to the aid of the *English Trader*, a freighter which had run aground on Hammond Knoll. Although RNLI boats were under the direction of the Naval base when going out on a mission, the Navy could only request, not order a launch.

Coxswain Blogg was then 65 years old. He had been coxswain of the Cromer boat since 1909 and had joined the crew as far back as 1894. He had won the RNLI gold medal three times. Only one other man has done this – Sir Richard Hillary, the Institution's founder. One gold medal was awarded to Blogg for the rescue of the *SS Fernebo* in 1917. The second for his service to the *SS Georgia,* a tanker which split in two off Cromer in 1927. The third gold was won on 5th August 1941, only ten weeks before the *English Trader* mission when the Cromer lifeboat took off 88 survivors, out of 119 rescued men from six ships which grounded on the Haisboroughs when sailing as part of Convoy FS 559.

The two years of war had been hectic for the Cromer lifeboatmen as so many fighter and bomber airfields were sited inland of the station and aircraft in difficulty, returning from raids over Occupied Europe, often came down in the North Sea. The lifeboat was called to search for survivors in all weathers. Seeking a small dinghy in a waste of rough water was often a forlorn task and on many a bitter night the crew of the *H F Bailey*, Cromer's motor-lifeboat, were out seeking airmen, but had to return chilled to the marrow, heavy-hearted and empty-handed.

On this Sunday morning, Henry Blogg accepted the responsibility of launching, for during the war, Major E T Hansell, the Honorary Secretary, was serving in the Forces. The *H F Bailey's* 12-man crew consisted of:

Coxswain – Henry G Blogg
Second Coxswain – John J Davies, Sen

Mechanic – Henry W Davies
Assistant Mechanic – James W Davies
Signalman – Edward W Allen
Bowman – William T Davies.
    Crewmen – John J Davies, Jnr; Sidney C Harrison; Henry T Davies; William H Davies; Robert C Davies and James H Davies

There were nine Davies' in the crew of twelve!

Within 15 minutes of the call the Cromer lifeboat had been launched. She was a 46ft Watson cabin type boat built by Groves and Guttridge of Cowes and stationed at Cromer since 1935. When she left in 1945 she had been launched 154 times and was the means of saving 448 lives. A predecessor of the same name had been placed at the station in 1923 when a shed was specially built at the end of the pier to house her.

Usually, she carried a crew of eight and these were assembled from various parts of the town, but this morning there were 12. Signalling the crew for a launch by means of maroons was not possible in wartime owing to confusion with gunfire. All men were not on the telephone so someone went round on a bicycle, or ran, to their homes. This took more time than the peacetime maroon system. Often, relatives followed the crew's mad dash to the boathouse with some item of clothing or seaboots which they had not waited to take. One man even pulled his trousers on over his pyjamas in his haste. In any case when the call comes for the lifeboat, every crewman drops whatever job he is doing and makes for the pier-end as fast as he can. A lot of other folk in the town, interested in their lifeboat, also hurry to the sea-front to see the launch.

On this Sunday, the quiet seaside town came suddenly to life. The boathouse at the pier's far end had been a boon to the station. It enabled a boat to run down its slipway into deep water. Previously of course, the craft had to be dragged on its carriage from its house at the bottom of the East Gangway over a rough beach and launched through the surf. The turmoil of breaking seas on the North Norfolk coast when the wind was in the north-east made this operation dangerous and difficult. One man had been crushed to death during a launch.

A previous boat, the pulling-and-sailing *Louisa Heartwell* had given wonderful service to the Institution and she was retained in No 2 shed – or the old boathouse. So efficient was the launching from the pier that on one occasion, from the time the message was received for the boat to launch to the time she actually slid down the slipway was four minutes. On this particular morning however, it was a much longer job – 15 minutes before the hammer struck the slip-pin and the boat was free of its cable. The released boat, under its own weight, launched into the rough sea creating a great bowl of spray, and was soon tussling with a full gale from the north-north-east.

This is the most uncomfortable quarter for the wind at Cromer. As there is no

Above, the English Trader *lying at anchor in Havana, Cuba. Below, diagram of the layout of the* English Trader.
Overleaf, the death throes of the English Trader, *taken from the lifeboat as the crew left their stricken ship.*

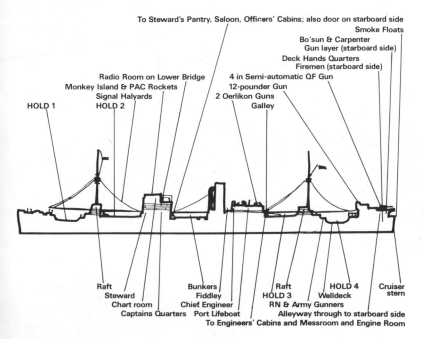

Cromer lifeboat, the H.F. Bailey.

Yarmouth and Gorleston lifeboat, the Louise Stephens.

land between the resort and the North Pole, the wind, sweeping over hundreds of miles of open sea, strikes this bit of England which projects almost defiantly into the North Sea. Following an unhindered path, the sea also builds up great rollers which break in a fury that must be seen to be believed.

One of the crew, James Davies, who was later drowned in a tragic fishing capsize, kept a record of his lifeboat services in a small exercise book and he describes this storm as a 'terrible north-east gale'. There were heavy squalls of hail which cut visibility to a few yards while they lasted. There was also rain and sleet and the sea was very rough. It was what is generally known as 'lifeboat weather'.

By 10 am, the *H F Bailey* had passed the North Haisborough buoy which meant she had steamed due east from Cromer to clear the Haisborough Sands. It was particularly rough here and the boat was smothered in spray as her bows cut the oncoming heavy waves and the gale flung the water back over the boat. She then veered south-east towards Hammond Knoll. With this sharp variation in course, the boat was running before the seas and the following waves were so boisterous that one of the crew stood-by in the stern ready to throw out the drogue, to steady the lifeboat if it became necessary – the drogue acting as a brake.

So, with short, steep seas baying at their heels like hounds, they reached the Knoll at 11.35 am and found the *English Trader* fast on the sands with most of her hull under water. One mast, the funnel and some of her superstructure were all that could be seen above the tumbling waters. The seas were raking her from end to end and it looked as if she had broken her back for'ard of the bridge. Of the six ships of Convoy FS 559 which had grounded on the nearby Haisborough Sands a few weeks earlier, every one broke its back!

In his 50 years' service with the lifeboats, Henry Blogg had seen many ships similarly stranded and he knew that the problem was the riot of seas that surrounded a wreck when wind and sea were roused in anger.

Sandbanks can be a boon to shipping as they afford some shelter during storms by breaking the force of the waves. Many vessels anchor and ride out a gale in Yarmouth Roads letting the Scroby Sands serve as a breakwater for them. When that is said, there is nothing else good about them. They confront a lifeboat coxswain with severe problems as the behaviour of the seas is unpredictable. In a storm, masses of water are set in motion by wind and tide and while moving freely through perhaps twenty fathoms of water or more, they are suddenly obstructed by a sand barrier, the volume of water is forced up and into the shallows with the result that it heaves and breaks out in all directions creating a confusion of currents. Freak seas, caused when waves come into head-on collision, make conditions that challenge the finest seaman or craft to survive.

Henry Blogg said later that the problem confronting him on the Knoll was the most appalling he had ever had to face. And throughout his action-filled life, the North Sea – the Haisborough Sands in particular – had set him many a puzzle. On the weather-side of the *English Trader*, the gale was causing seas to run along her flanks like terrified animals. And on the lee-side, which should have been more sheltered, the turmoil of currents and breaking seas made things almost as bad. At times, the waves came from two directions along the hull. One sea running along the weather-side from for'ard and another from aft would meet amidships and go up like a mine explosion. Some of these contending waves reached the top of the mast, and then fell back in a turmoil of hundreds of tons of water on the ship and immediately around it. One of the Cromer men said he had: 'never seen a ship in a worse predicament.'

No lifeboat could hope to lie alongside in such a situation. The possibility remained of getting a line aboard with the line-throwing pistol but this meant hauling each man from the wreck in the breeches-buoy to the lifeboat through boiling seas. It would certainly have meant casualties. The strain on the lifeboat itself, trying to hold station under such a test, would be tremendous. There was, however, no alternative.

When Henry Blogg made the statement about the problem he had to meet one must remember his veracity. He would not exaggerate conditions. Early in his career, his lawyer urged him in the witness-box to say the seas were rough. It was a salvage case and the claim hinged on that, but Henry Blogg would not say so. His lawyer, Henry Murrell of Yarmouth, grew annoyed with him and said: 'Surely, you would agree it was a rough sea?'

A slow smile spread over Blogg's face and then he said: 'Well, perhaps you would call it rough, but I wouldn't.'

He got a lecture from his lawyer later, but that did not bother him. So, if Blogg said the *English Trader* rescue set him the greatest problem of his long career – it was so.

Charles Johnson, coxswain of the Great Yarmouth and Gorleston lifeboat for 12 years, as well as William Hickson, who was actually on the ship itself, confirm the headache the North Sea set the rescuers.

Henry 'Shrimp' Davies, now retired from his post as coxwain of the Cromer lifeboat, was one of the younger members of the crew on that memorable Sunday. He says he saw the spray from the converging, clashing seas going right over the masts. His brother, Jimmy called them: 'terrific seas'.

To add to the hazards of the rescue the sea had plundered all four holds and had scoured much of the cargo from them so that the water around was a jumble of flotsam. Moreover, baulks of timber were floating about and the ship's derricks, used for loading and unloading cargo, had broken free and were swinging with each movement of the ship and when caught by a surge of water.

The *H F Bailey* hove-to midway between the stern of the destroyer and the wreck. She stood off well clear of both ships and the bank. Coxswain Blogg tried to weigh up the situation. At last he signalled that he would move in closer to see if there was a way in which to tackle what looked to be an impossible task.

From the bridge of the *English Trader*, officers and men watched the preparations on the lifeboat for a line-gun attempt. The yellow oilskins and sou'westers showed against the dark background of sea and stormy sky as they took positions on the deck while their boat plunged and reared like a spirited colt.

At 1.15 pm the Cromer boat moved forward, her bows slicing the seas. Then with her engines exerting more power, a cloud of spray enveloped her completely. A signal lamp flashed the message: 'Stand by for line.'

On the wreck, the chief mate focussed his binoculars on the lifeboat. He identified it and called over his shoulder to the captain: 'It's the Cromer lifeboat!'

'Yes,' answered Captain Grimstone as if he had already decided that himself.

'Cromer?' queried one of the sailors. 'Where's that?'

'Norfolk,' came the reply.

'Oh,' exclaimed the seaman as if the information still left him no wiser.

'All right, lads,' interrupted the captain briskly. 'Get yourselves sorted out and stand by to catch the line when it comes aboard.'

On destroyer and steamer all eyes were fixed on the *H F Bailey* as she closed the gap to the wreck. Her blue and white paintwork showed up distinctly as if it had been newly painted – there was certainly no dust on it! Perhaps the sun, peeping through a rare break in the clouds brightened the scene. Anyhow, to the mariners on the bridge she made a brave sight as they watched her dipping deep into the trough of a sea, then with bows rearing upwards, climb the crest of the next wave. As she drove hard against the sea, her port gunwale was under the boiling white backwash which looked as if it would bury the small craft. But her wooden hull was packed to capacity with water-tight aircases giving her a buoyancy no other craft could match. Tests before her commissioning had confirmed her amazing ability to take on the seas, shed them through her scuppers, and even if half buried in water, still to bounce up like a cork and ride on.

One of the lifeboatmen could be seen steadying himself by the canopy amidships, holding the line-throwing pistol. A cloud of spray lifted over the bows as she cleared through the salty crest of a sea which folded over resembling a huge, moving snowdrift. The *H F Bailey* seemed to shake herself of the water like a terrier emerging from a pond.

With her engines thrusting powerfully, the *H F Bailey* forged upwind until she was ahead of the bridge of the wreck and about twenty yards from her.

Signalman Edward 'Boy Primo' Allen waited for Henry Blogg's command to fire the gun. For Blogg it was a critical moment as he had to use his engines to hold the lifeboat head-on to the erratic sea and at the same time give his signalman the right angle to fire and not overshoot the bridge of the *English Trader*.

'Boy Primo' was watching the bridge of the steamer as well as the upraised arm of his skipper and as the arm dropped, there was a shouted command: 'Fire!'

The seamen on the wreck saw a puff of smoke as the pistol was fired and the steel projectile, carrying a fifty-fathom line from a canister, sped straight towards them on the ship. They were out along the wing of the bridge, waiting to catch the line and secure it. But neither the bolt nor the line reached them. Instead the steel shaft suddenly curved upwards and over in a complete loop only a few yards short of the ship. The gale-force wind had caught it and, overcoming its velocity, turned it away from its target.

'Too much wind,' remarked Captain Grimstone. 'Never mind. We may have better luck next time.'

The lifeboat carried on past the firing point. There was no question of a tight turn with the crates and barrels bobbing about, so she swept out over the Knoll in a wide arc and returned for a second attempt. It was nearly ten minutes before the *H F Bailey* was able to fire a second time to put a line on the one and only place where the seamen could take it. Again it was unsuccessful – this time the line falling well short of the ship. Once more the boat turned away from the wreck.It would be suicide to try and get closer or stay longer. The seamen were disappointed but they could see only too clearly the risks involved for the Cromer men.

Coxswain Blogg, speaking to his second coxswain, agreed that with the dropping of the tide, possibly in an hour or so, the sea would be less ferocious and it might give them the opportunity to move in closer and get the line over the bridge. He felt that, at present, the risks to both his crew and boat were too great. The odds were heavily against him.

He took his boat off the bank into deep water, but not to anchor. Instead, the coxswain 'dodged about', keeping the boat head-on to the waves. And 'Boy Primo' signalled the *English Trader:* 'We will wait for slack water.'

The destroyer was also informed of Blogg's decision. Slack water would occur about 4 pm and last about two hours. It was the period between the tides when the flow of water is reduced. For all vessels concerned, it was now a case of waiting to see if conditions did ameliorate as hoped.

CHAPTER 6
'Knockdown'

 FOR OVER an hour the Cromer boat reared and plunged, maintaining her head to the seas. Although off the bank and in deep water, with the seas running true it was a test of seamanship, but Blogg had done it many times before.

From the bridge of the steamer, time and time again, the lifeboat appeared to be buried in spindrift and spray beneath big billows and even the truck at her masthead was lost to sight. Then it would appear with the bows pointing high and water cascading from her decks – all her scuppers spouting as she rid herself of the burden taken on with the last sea.

During that period of waiting the qualities of seamanship and character of coxswain and crew were fully tried. But as time dragged past in discomfort, it became more and more nerve-racking. Patience sorely tested. Some of the younger members became restless and wanted to get on with the job. With an occasional suggestion they urged their coxswain to make another attempt. It was understandable – they had been on the dashing, dramatic rescue to Convoy FS 559 only a few weeks previously and had seen the masterly way Blogg had twice without hesitation driven their boat right on to the decks of two nearly-submerged, grounded steamers. By so doing he had rescued 16 men from *SS Oxshott,* and 19 from the *SS Deerwood*.

Henry Blogg listened to their comments and without making a reply kept watching the seas. He knew only too well from what he had already seen and experienced that although the sea had been rough on Haisborough at the time of the Convoy rescue, conditions were far worse here. From the time he had been a lad at school and gone fishing with his longshoremen relatives, he had known the sea in its many moods. As a fisherman and a lifeboatman he was sea-wary. His judgment told him that his opportunity for this rescue had not come.

'No,' he said at last, shaking his head, 'we'll do more harm than good.'

His second coxswain agreed with him and Blogg turned away to watch an oncoming sea. Several minutes passed sluggishly, minutes filled with action and decision for a few of the crew, coxswain and mechanics particularly, but for the others, there was little to do but wait in discomfort. Again hints were made that they might now have another try to get a line aboard. Henry Blogg himself thought the seas were somewhat less heavy, and swayed by some of his young crew he decided to make the trial.

It is the only time this strong-willed man gave way to pressure against what he really knew was sound judgment. When he set his mind on a course of action he could be more stubborn than the proverbial mule. 'Awkward,' some men said.

Anyway, he was quite indifferent to what others thought of him or what he was doing. If he did not want to talk about a rescue to reporters or enquirers, wild horses would not drag a sentence out of him. Undoubtedly, this decision to make the trial remained one of the big regrets in a long life-saving career.

At 2.15 pm Blogg gave his mechanics the order to move: 'Slow ahead.' The *H F Bailey* headed towards the lee-side of the casualty. In making this approach over the bank, it was necessary for the lifeboat to turn broadside to the sea and she was doing this when, in the coxswain's own words: 'We were trying to approach at half-speed, and when still about 100 yards away a huge wall of water suddenly rose up on our port side. There was a shout: "Look out!" and before I could even give a half-turn to the wheel – to meet the oncoming sea – I was lifted out of the boat just as though I had been a bit of cork.

'We were simply overwhelmed by the sheer weight of water. How the boat righted herself I should never understand. It must indeed have been the hand of Providence. The boat must have been hit hardest abaft the fore cockpit. Had she been hit as hard along her whole length, there would be no lifeboat crew in Cromer today.'

William Hickson, watching intently with his comrades from the *English Trader*, saw the Cromer boat move in for what he assumed to be another attempt to get a line to them. He said that at the moment when the *H F Bailey* lay deep in a trough, almost hidden from his view: 'A particularly large sea swept across the bows of the *English Trader*. It was moving at a tremendous speed and rolling high with very little white showing at its summit. It was silent and huge as it seemed to glide past the bridge, heading for the edge of the sandbank and deeper water. It was also running straight towards where the lifeboat was. The bearing to the wreck was about 130° port, 170° starboard.'

As the wave passed by the bridge where the 44 seamen were grouped, another wave broke in thundering white fury across the midship decks. It reached halfway up the funnel, churning and throwing up clouds of spray. It powered on and the two mountainous masses of water met near the edge of the sandbank. With a thunderous roar they collided and joined in one massive eruption.

Somewhere behind the grey-green hill of water with its leaping crest was the Cromer boat. Suddenly the seamen saw it – beam-on to the sea. It was leaning over to starboard at a perilous angle and was being swept forward broadside-on.

Captain Grimstone said later: 'I saw her keel come right out of the water.'

Two of the *English Trader* crewmen standing at the extreme end of the bridge with the best view of the scene, suddenly cried out: 'The lifeboat's turned over!'

The mate who was standing close behind, leapt forward pointing: 'My God – there are men in the water!'

In the midst of that immense breaking wave, five lifeboatmen struggled. Other seamen on the wreck confirmed what Captain Grimstone said, that the *H F Bailey's* keel came clear of the water. She hovered in this position for a fraction of a minute as though undecided whether to go completely over, and then slowly righted herself, water gushing and cascading around her. A few more inches and she would have turned turtle in complete disaster. The *H F Bailey* was not a self-righting craft and she would have stayed upside down. In that wild sea all her crew must have drowned, for there was nothing the *English Trader* or the destroyer could do to save them.

The following were all swept clean overboard: Coxswain Henry Blogg who could not swim despite all his life spent in inshore fishing and lifeboats; the second coxswain Jack Davies; his nephew Henry 'Shrimp' Davies; Sid Harrison and Edward 'Boy Primo' Allen. Two other members of the crew also went overboard, but managed to grab the guard-rails and haul themselves back into the boat. Every man abaft of midships had gone over the side.

After being carried through most of the broken water, Henry Blogg opened his eyes and was amazed to see the *H F Bailey* had regained her balance. 'Shrimp' Davies was caught by the sea and actually felt the guard-rail under him as he was swept off his feet. He did not grab it as the other two men had done for even in the split second of the sea holding him in its grasp, he thought: The boat is going right over. If I grab this rail I shall be covered with it.

He felt a terrific sensation of cold as he was plunged into the sea. Then he found himself with his head above water. His kapok-filled lifebelt kept his head up. Choking and retching with the salt water he had swallowed, he could not see the lifeboat. He was certain she had gone right over. Then he was suddenly aware of a sou'wester and upraised arm – another man was close to him in the trough of a sea. It was Sid Harrison. Sid had grabbed at the wireless mast as the wave hit him but the sea was too powerful and broke his hold.

The two men did not swim but were washed towards each other and when close they clutched involuntarily at one another. Yet even as one grasped the other, each man realised that it could be fatal and together, as though by an unspoken, mutual agreement, they released their grip. Henry Davies, spitting and gulping, managed to say: 'This is a bad end, Sid.'

Then he added as his thoughts turned to something else: 'Have you got your boots off?'

'Yes,' gasped Sid. 'I lost mine when I came over. Have you?' Being wartime, fishermen found it difficult to get the right-sized seaboots and Sid's were a bit large so that they had come off of their own account.

Henry's were a better fit. 'No,' he spluttered, apparently aware for the first time that he was still cumbered with his boots. 'I've still got mine on.'

He at once began thrusting with the toe of one boot against the heel of the other to rid himself of them. Years later he recalled what a struggle it was and says it must have taken him three or four minutes of kicking and pushing. He began to think he would never get them off but after several sharp, almost savage kicks he at last was free of both boots. He felt more buoyant straightaway. But the cold was nearly unbearable. It seemed to be eating right into him. There had been squalls of sleet and hail only a few minutes earlier.

Sid Harrison was saying something to 'Shrimp' which he could not catch because of the noise about him, when a wave lifted them high and the two men were parted. Sid said afterwards: 'I had to go where the waves took me. I tried to get hold of a crate, but could not hold on.'

With merely his head and shoulders above the water, surrounded by little moving hills of water, Henry Davies was unable to see either the *H F Bailey* or the wreck. He still felt convinced that the lifeboat had capsized. Despite having rid himself of his seaboots, and struggle as he might to keep his head above the water, it was so broken, surging and splashing about him that he felt his lungs were bursting. One sea went right over him, pushing him down and down. He came to the surface coughing and choking. The buoyancy of his lifebelt had brought him up. But a sensation of utter despair came over him. He thought there was no point in trying to keep afloat. This brutal green sea would just tease and torture him. It would be useless to fight against it but merely prolong the agony as it filled his lungs with salt water and drove the last breath from his body. He was beyond reach of any help. There were ships and men somewhere about on this bank but they, like himself, were in dire straits. He might just as well give up and end the misery of it all.

His whole body felt numb, legs and arms were unresponsive. The cold was paralysing. A jumbled, half-formed prayer went through his mind. Then he was conscious of being lifted high as a curling wave raised him on its crest as if to deliberately let him see about him, and there, his red bleared eyes saw across the tumbling water the *English Trader* and also, even more hope-restoring, was the *H F Bailey* – the right way up!

At that precise moment someone on the lifeboat saw him as he was raised above the concealing troughs of the waves. That big sea bringing him into view the moment after his unuttered prayer was made, saved his life. His mates still on the *H F Bailey*, now began manoeuvring the boat towards him. 'Shrimp' was not to drown on Hammond Knoll but to survive and succeed Henry Blogg as coxswain in 1947.

It was fortunate that the sea in that particular part of the Hammond Knoll, 100 yards from the freighter, was less littered with wreckage than was strewn elsewhere.

As the *H F Bailey* slowly, unwillingly righted herself with five of her crew in the water and two others clambering desperately back on board over the rails, W H Davies picked himself up from the deck where he had been flung. He had been saved by the guard-rail from also going overboard. Taking in the situation, as the boat righted, he staggered over the swilling deck to the helm. Although dazed and winded by the blow he had taken, he grasped the wheel and as both engines were running, he called out: 'Full astern,' to the mechanics.

He could see Henry Blogg and also his father, Jack Davies in the water close by. He endeavoured to bring the lifeboat towards them, all the while watching the big seas around. Then one of the crew remembered an aircraft dinghy that was stowed under the canopy. Two or three of them dragged it out and flung it over the side to Henry Blogg. He grasped it and held on. Then he reached back with one hand and clasped the fingers of his second coxswain who was hauled first on board.

The words 'hauled on board' convey little of the difficulty of getting a man who has been thrown into the sea back on board a lifeboat. It always has and still is a major problem of life-saving at sea. Apart from the weight of the man, the sodden clothing, seaboots and oilskins, his kapok-filled lifebelt projecting from his chest, catches under the deep bulge of the lifeboat fender. He has to be lifted three or four feet despite the low freeboard of the lifeboat. Moreover, the man in the water is often practically incapable of doing anything to help himself. Possibly he has been struck by a big sea, winded or half stunned and shocked by immersion in cold water.

On the *H F Bailey*, one of the rescuers, W H Davies, had been knocked down by the sea and two others had been swept overboard and had managed to get back on board themselves, but most of the breath in their bodies had been knocked out of them. Fortunately, the *H F Bailey* was carrying a full crew and with the seven men left on board, although one was at the wheel and two at the engines, they managed to get Jack Davies back into the lifeboat.

He said later: 'When I got on board, I put two fingers on the back of my tongue and got rid of some of the sea-water.'

While those that could help were trying to get the men into the boat, W H Davies was endeavouring to keep the *H F Bailey* near to the aircraft dinghy to which Henry Blogg was clinging. When they got alongside the dinghy they hauled the coxswain on board. He flopped on the deck and had to be helped to his feet. Somehow he made his way, bent almost double, to the wheel. He clung on to the cabin for two or three minutes gagging with the water he had swallowed and fighting to regain his breath. Then, as he began to feel better, he took over the helm.

While this was occurring the rest of the crew were endeavouring to locate the other three men in the sea, but a man's head is easily hidden in a confused sea and the three men could have been carried in various directions. With Henry Blogg feeling stronger, W H Davies also went to the side looking for the rest of the crew. Five minutes passed, then Henry Davies was spotted by three men simultaneously as a wave lifted him. The boat was taken towards him and when the *H F Bailey* was on the crest of a wave, a crewman coiled a rope and threw it with such accuracy that it landed on 'Shrimp's' chest, and in a moment he had wound it round both hands and wrists and even gripped it with his teeth. He was pulled in over the side still gripping the line.

It was the turn of Sid Harrison. He was also brought in with a line and the two were given a tot of rum, but Sid had swallowed so much water it came up again. Both men were so water-logged it took four or five minutes to stop their teeth chattering.

When the last man, Signalman Allen was seen, he had been carried farthest from the lifeboat and was unconscious when they reached him. His lifejacket was keeping his head out of the water, but he was a dead weight and although four men helped to get him aboard they were so exhausted that one of the mechanics was called to help. 'Boy Primo' was heaved over the rails and laid on the swilling deck. He had been twenty-five minutes in that bitterly cold sea.

They knelt beside him with the spray flying over them as they rubbed and chafed his hands and face trying to revive him. Gradually the 49-year-old signalman responded and stirred. More vigorous rubbing and slapping and his eyes opened. He tried to raise himself up. Someone put an arm under him and helped him into a sitting position and muttering something about his mittens, he started pulling one on. They were of course fastened by ribbons to his oilskins but had been dragged off his hands in the water. He spoke a few incoherent words and suddenly dropped back onto the deck. Comrades lifted him up and carried him aft and laid him down continuing to apply artificial respiration and massage. Again he seemed to respond but once more he collapsed.

On the *English Trader*, the disaster to the *H F Bailey* upset every seaman. It was half an hour of deep anxiety and concern. They knew the plight of the Cromer men resulted from their eagerness to succour them. The dismay at seeing the men struggling in the water, and the roll over of the boat itself, was followed by rising hopes when the lifeboat righted herself and they could see that she was being brought under control. They saw what they thought was a buoy thrown to someone in the sea. They saw him cling to it and catch hold of another lifeboatman. They felt keen frustration at their own inability to render any assistance in this crisis – they could just watch and flinch as the spray hit them. Whether or not the men in the sea were saved or drowned, they could not affect the issue. Some of them prayed for their rescue as the minutes ticked away and there were still three men unrescued. The compassion that had prompted the lifeboatmen to answer the distress call now prompted these hardened sailors to pray that they would survive; that they might make that extra effort despite the numbness that the cold water must induce, to hold on until they could be reached.

Like spectators on a touch-line willing the players on the field to extra effort, so these seamen willed their strength across the hostile water to the men whose strength, under shock and exposure, must be failing.

They saw Henry Blogg and Jack Davies and then 'Shrimp' lifted aboard. The line thrown to Sid Harrison fell short and they watched him swim slowly towards it, and as they saw him grip the rope the mate gave a heartfelt: 'Ah, good lad. He's got it!'

Another long sea boiled over the sandbank near them, obscuring the lifeboat from the view of the shipwrecked men. When it passed and the spray cleared, Sid was seen clinging to the starboard ratlines of the boat. He had been pulled in by the line.

Watching Blogg bring the *H F Bailey* round sharply they guessed someone else had been spotted and presently another man, Signalman Allen was briefly glimpsed through the heaving, intervening water. Through binoculars they saw he was not trying to swim or struggle and they guessed he must be in very poor shape. But they watched him being lifted aboard by a group of lifeboatmen and laid on the deck. They surmised from the long time he had been immersed that his condition must be critical. But the fact that all the men thrown out of the *H F Bailey* had been recovered was little short of a miracle in the seas then running. They had seen three of their own company snatched to their deaths in seconds and yet all the men from the *H F Bailey* were back on board. Most of these sailors had sailed in seas around the world and seen the sea in varying moods so they appreciated the skill that the Cromer crew had shown in a time of disaster in recovering from the knockdown.

The Institution has built hundreds of splendid boats in its long history. Neither money nor effort have been spared to make them sturdy, stable and as buoyant as possible but there is still no perfectly safe lifeboat. It is questionable if there ever will be. All the more credit to the men who go out in them.

There is little doubt that the recovery of five men from that sea was possible because the boat itself had shown remarkable stability when the wave hit it. This stability surprised her crew, especially her famous coxswain. Nonetheless, the quick action and clear thinking of the men left on board in the crisis had effected a fine rescue. Had the sea swept the boat and men different ways during those first few minutes, their recovery would have been much more difficult if not impossible.

An armchair critic might ask if there was any slackness or foolhardiness on the part of Henry Blogg or his men? The recent capsize and knockdown of three modern lifeboats clearly shows that the disaster could happen to the most vigilant crew. The colliding waves that rolled the *H F Bailey* onto her beam-end could not be anticipated. They were freak waves. The suddenness and surprise of this accident was their undoing. Although Henry Blogg had moved in from the deep water against his better judgment, there was no negligence on his part or his men.

This grim incident illustrates only too well the hazards that are there in a rescue on a shoal, particularly in such foul weather conditions. This element of surprise freak seas is not a feature of past years – recent disasters to modern lifeboats show what can happen.*

The knockdown of the *H F Bailey* was a setback to the wrecked seamen. To one another they spoke of their concern for the Cromer men. The lifeboat looked so small, dwarfed by the waves as she reared and plunged on them as if riding some fantastic watery switchback. Although hardly any of the men had ever needed a lifeboat, they knew that this was no ordinary mission, for the odds were stacked against such a small craft in these big seas. The evidence of what the sea could do, even to a specially built craft, they had just witnessed. What it could do to their far larger vessel was happening before their eyes.

Even if a line was secured from lifeboat to wreck they still had to cross that perilous gap with unpredictable waves coming in from all angles. They had seen three of their mates thrown about by seas and the dangers that lay in swinging in a breeches-buoy between ship and boat were unpleasant to think upon. But no one spoke of it.

On the *H F Bailey*, once all the crew were back in her, there were plenty of problems. The first was to help 'Boy Primo' whose condition was critical. He had not recovered consciousness and his breathing was very slight. There was a faint pulse response. Although a strong man, his long immersion had taken heavy toll. There was no mark of a blow on him caused by the wave that carried him out of the boat. It must have lifted him clear of the rails. And he had not, apparently, been struck by any of the floating objects around the wreck.

Although it was not now snowing on the Knoll, at that time it was on the nearby coast and the sea was icy cold. Henry Blogg himself felt so weak after his own much shorter time in the water that he had difficulty turning the wheel although he insisted on keeping the helm. To make matters worse the *H F Bailey* was not responding to the starboard engine or the wheel as she should have done. Evidently a rope had been washed overboard and entangled itself around the propeller shaft. This did not stop the propeller from turning but acted as a brake and much reduced its effectiveness. When it was eventually hacked away, piece by piece, it was found to be an inch and a half bearing line.

All hope therefore, of doing any more for the shipwrecked men was out of the question. It was 3 pm. The lifeboatmen had been out seven hours and most of them were exhausted. Henry Blogg decided, after a word with his crew, to make for Yarmouth. There was no possibility of returning to Cromer which would have taken longer anyway running into the gale and it was not possible to rehouse the *H F Bailey* or get the sick man ashore.

One disadvantage to set against the many advantages of the boathouse at the

*See Note 3, p 96.

end of the pier was that whereas in normal seas, the boat could be manoeuvred, with the aid of a fixed buoy to be hauled stern first up the slipway into her house, in rough seas this could not be done. The only alternative was to run the boat down to Yarmouth where she must wait at the Gorleston jetty for the weather to moderate, when the crew could bring her back to Cromer.

The men on the *English Trader* were not surprised therefore, and not dismayed when they saw the *H F Bailey* signal to the destroyer and turn her bows away from the Knoll. They saw a figure on the fore-deck raise an arm and a faint shout carried through the howl of the wind: 'We'll be back.'

At least, they caught the word 'back' and rightly assumed that 'We'll be back,' was the message intended.

They watched a signal lamp flashing on *HMS Vesper* and Arthur Lond, the second mate, read it, repeating each word aloud as he deciphered the message: 'The Cromer lifeboat crew are in some distress. Signalman very ill. Regret they must return to harbour.'

The sea had won the first round. Triumphantly it continued smashing up the *English Trader*.

CHAPTER 7
The Yarmouth and Gorleston Lifeboat Launches

 FOLLOWING THE disaster to the Cromer boat and Henry Blogg's decision to head for Yarmouth to get the sick man to hospital – and also allow the rest of his crew to recuperate from their ordeal, the Great Yarmouth and Gorleston lifeboat station was called upon to help. Her boat, the ON820 *Louise Stephens,* was also a 46ft East Coast non-self-righting type with a 4'6″ draught and fitted with two VE4 Ferry engines. She was built at Cowes by J S White and company and had been at Gorleston since 1939 where she remained until 1967, having launched 305 times and rescued 177 lives.

Her coxswain, Charles Johnson, had served as skipper since February 1934. He retired in December 1946, and died in 1957. Apart from being coxswain of the *Louise Stephens,* Charles Johnson was a drifter skipper at Yarmouth and also kept the Waterside Tavern on Gorleston quay. He was a big man, weighing 18 stone. His fishing experience gave him a sound knowledge of the seas around the busy port and the treacherous sands of Scroby. His thorough knowledge of the area was shortly to be tested to the full. Like Henry Blogg he was most reticent about his lifeboat work. Press reporters could get very little out of him after a rescue. His boat was kept in the lifeboathouse on Gorleston quay.

On Sunday, 26th October, with a full NNE gale blowing, several of the Yarmouth crew had gathered at the boathouse. There were a few jobs to be done to the *Louise Stephens,* and it was the sort of weather when the boat might be needed.

The men, all fishermen or tugmen, were discussing the gale and the rough seas and the movement of various vessels, for there was always plenty of activity in that busy harbour, particularly in wartime. George Mobbs, the first mechanic who later became coxswain, was working on some part of an engine when Coxswain Johnson was seen hurrying along the cobbled quay fighting the wind. Entering the house he said somewhat breathlessly to John Wright, his second coxswain: 'Jack, Cromer is off this morning. There's a big 'un on Hammond Knoll. A really big ship.'

The coxswain had been notified by the coastguard as part of the back-up system of informing flanking stations of a launch, so that they could give cover when the other craft was on a service. He added: 'She must be a big ship to get on the Knoll. There's plenty of water there.'

Jack Wright was also a drifter and trawler skipper. He said: 'Yes, but there is a patch where they could touch.'

Joe – as Charles Johnson was nicknamed – shook his head decisively. Although he had never been called to a casualty on the Knoll, he disagreed. 'No, no, Jack,' he said.

The two drifter skippers began arguing about the depth of water on the sandbank and after a time decided to settle the matter by consulting the charts. So the men not doing any particular job went into the lookout and took out the relevant coastal maps. Jack Wright pointed to a spot on the chart and said: 'That's where she must be.'

The two men then began to lay a course off for this spot just in case they should be needed. It was as well they did so – it saved time later, for an hour afterwards the telephone rang and George Mobbs, the mechanic, answered it. The call was from the Yarmouth Naval base informing them that the Cromer boat was encountering very bad conditions and requesting them to reinforce her at the scene of the wreck.

George Mobbs laid down the receiver and, turning to his coxswain said: 'We shall soon know now where she is. We've got to go.'

He handed the telephone to the coxswain who spoke with the naval officer and told him he would launch within a few minutes. It was then 11.40 am.

Everyone jumped into action. Some men dashed home to get gear and notify relatives they were off on a mission. Others got the engines running and everything ready for the launch. The flanking stations of Lowestoft and Caister were notified of developments by the coastguard.

At noon the *Louise Stephens* slid down her slipway into the churned, heaving water of the harbour as the boom, consisting of heavy timbers studded with long spikes, was winched open to let her pass into Yarmouth Roads.

The crew consisted of:

Coxswain – Charles Johnson, Drifter skipper
Second Coxswain – John Wright, Drifter and trawler skipper
Signalman – William Parker, Drifterman
Mechanic – George Mobbs, full-time lifeboatman
Assistant Mechanic – Arthur Bush, Drifterman
Bowman – Thomas Morley, Drifterman
Crewman – Lewis Symonds, Tugman on the *George Jewson*.

The very difficult 22-mile journey in the face of the strong northerly gale began. Rough seas and a flood tide made matters worse. The Yarmouth men had to fight all the way. In the words of George Mobbs: 'It was a heavy slog.'

Running northwards through the Barley Picle and the Cockle Gat, they veered westward to pass round the end of the South Haisborough Sands and then north-eastwards to Hammond Knoll. As they thrust towards the sandbank, George Mobbs picked up on the radio telephone, a call from the *H F Bailey* mechanic, Henry 'Swank' Davies who said he had been trying to call the Yarmouth Naval base and had not been able to make contact. He asked: 'Can you bring a doctor with you? 'Boy Primo' is in a bad way.'

George gave his skipper the message and Charles Johnson said: 'Tell them we are well on our way and will soon be nearing the casualty. We can't turn back now but will pass on the message for a doctor and ambulance to be at Yarmouth quay.'

This was done as the *Louise Stephens* continued to the Knoll.

It took three and a half hours plunging into heavy seas with spray flying over the masts and the decks continuously awash before they sighted the wreck. It was then 3.30 pm. The *English Trader* was roughly in the position predicted by Jack Wright, so his fishing navigation and experience had stood him in good stead! They also saw the sleek grey shape of *HMS Vesper* anchored in deep water. The *H F Bailey* had left the bank half an hour before so the two boats had passed but had not seen each other.

Coxswain Johnson moved in to the wreck as close as he dared to decide his best tactics. He knew that for the first time anyone could remember, the Cromer boat had been rolled onto her beam-ends in a near capsize and extreme caution was needed lest the same thing happen to this boat. He too, found conditions on the sandbank as Blogg had said: 'Truly appalling.'

Although the steamer had broken her back just for'ard of the bridge, she was not in two pieces, but a huge crack showed from the rails of her fore-deck almost to the waterline. The battering of the seas had apparently scoured away sand and shingle from under the vessel's bows so that her forward end was suspended over a great hole, and the strain of the pounding waves, rolling in with the main swell of the sea on her lee-side, caused her to crack open. On the weather-side, the pressure of the gale-force wind was supplemented by the confused seas. Seamen could be seen on the bridge and in the doorway of the chartroom. There was a heavy squall of rain and hail even as Coxswain Johnson told Jack Wright: 'We'll have to dodge about for a time. We can't get to her yet.'

So they stood off 'steaming' around in wide circles for half an hour. It was now slack water. The tide was at its lowest and Johnson knew it would give him his best chance of getting alongside; as less water was flowing on the bank and around the ship, so the bulk of the stranded ship would afford him more shelter on her lee-side. He decided to go in on the crest of a big sea and put a line aboard. Signalman Billy Parker prepared the gun. It was a Martin-Henry rifle which had been converted for line-throwing. Its steel butt gave a kick like a mule but it could be aimed accurately. Billy was a drifterman and a good marksman. In fact, he was sometimes accused of using that skill for a spot of night-poaching, but this he stoutly denied. The rifle took a blank cartridge and fired a projectile to which was affixed a thin hemp line the end of which would carry a stouter mooring rope.

On the wreck, the men saw Johnson was adopting a different tactic to Blogg for he took his boat further onto the sandbank until it was nearly out of sight in the spray and spindrift, then he was seen to turn a quarter of a mile ahead on the port bow. William Hickson said there were comments of admiration from his shipmates on the way the *Louise Stephens* was handled. They forgot their own predicament as they saw the Yarmouth boat ride on the head of a comber towards them. The lifeboat looked like an Australian surf-rider, held steady and on even keel but moving fast to them. They saw the lifeboatmen on her deck, and near the fore-mast a crouching figure, the signalman clinging with one hand to a rail and holding a gun in the other. Another man, half bent was beside him. Just for a moment it seemed the lifeboat was coming too close to the wreck and stood in danger of being carried into it by the sea, but then she was seen to slip back into the following trough, no doubt with her engines put 'astern'. It was so efficiently done it might have been standard practice.

As the boat came almost abeam of the *English Trader*, there was a puff of smoke. The men on the wreck, waiting to take the line, heard the whistle of the projectile as it travelled over their heads and the steel shaft landed with a clatter on the Monkey Island, the highest point of the superstructure. The line was aboard. In a trice it was grasped and held fast by eager hands.

Captain Grimstone barked: 'Hold it. Don't pull it. Wait for the signal.'

Coxswain Johnson's tactic had worked. The line was on the wreck. He had shouted orders – orders had to be shouted with the noise of wind and sea contending – to his mechanics: 'Slow ahead. Hold her. Go astern.'

George Mobbs and Arthur 'Pim' Bush responded as quickly as they could so that their engines should hold the craft as steady as the powerful seas would permit. As the line was caught on the wreck the lifeboatmen bent a three-inch mooring rope to it. This was pulled across the gap and secured. The lifeboat was hauled near the wreck. This was a position of danger, for the freighter's derricks were swinging at times and the sea carried large boxes which could crash into the wooden hull of the *Louise Stephens*. Nevertheless, it did seem that the moment of rescue had come and what the Cromer boat had tried to do when the tide was higher, they had accomplished.

But here on the Knoll at this time, the sea was master. Before the breeches-buoy could be affixed – or as one Yarmouth crewman erroneously thought, they might even get close enough for the wrecked men to swing down the loose ropes where the ship's wrecked lifeboat had hung, into the *Louise Stephens* – the mooring rope parted. The strain of the seas bouncing back from the wreck's hull and hitting the lifeboat was too great. The *Louise Stephens* lurched away. The skill of Coxswain Johnson had almost succeeded.

The lifeboatmen, who thought they were near enough for the seamen to swing down the davit ropes did not realise that three men had already been swept to their deaths trying to cross the bunker-deck which lay between the bridge and the boat-deck.

The period of slack water lasted some two hours and in that interval Charles Johnson, knowing this was the time of opportunity made no less than five separate attempts to get his boat near the wreck. With the second effort it seemed that they had again got into a place to haul up to the *English Trader*, almost within a biscuit toss, but again the sea would not have it.

When they made the fourth attempt the tide was 'shooting' (increasing) and they nearly met disaster – a similar or even worse fate than their sister lifeboat. While they were jockeying to get close into the freighter, a big wave swept clean over the *English Trader*, aft of the bridge. It hit the *Louise Stephens* on her starboard side with a blow like a heavyweight boxer's punch. She heeled right over on to her beam-ends. George Mobbs had deliberately wedged one foot against a vent-pipe and when the Coxswain yelled: 'Full astern!' the tilt of the boat did not throw him off balance and he set this throttle control with desperate urgency. His starboard engine roared in response, but it made no difference to the boat – the *Louise Stephens* was on her side at such an angle that the propeller was completely out of the water and racing in air.

'Another little push,' said the mechanic, 'and she must have capsized.'

Tom Morley, the bowman, was against the cockpit gripping the windscreen when the wave hit them and the boat heeled. It flung him clean over the screen into the cockpit on top of the two mechanics. Fortunately, the disaster that had struck the Cromer boat had warned the *Louise Stephens'* crew and every man was on the look-out for such a knockdown. They were holding to anything secure, or braced like George Mobbs, wherever possible, so that no man went overboard. The port engine responded to the coxswain's command and the boat sluggishly rolled back to an even keel, the starboard propeller also bit the water and the lifeboat moved clear of the wreck.

For the final attempt, the *Louise Stephens* made a run in and when nearing the casualty, her engines were throttled back so that she ceased her forward rush and lay almost in a deep trough, her stern beginning to rise on the following wave. When thirty or forty feet away the gun was again fired and the projectile hissed over the ship. The line was taken. But, as if wind and wave were intent on asserting themselves, a sea curled up into a long high wave with the gale behind it and, travelling fast between the wreck and the lifeboat, snatched the line from the hands that held it on the lifeboat. In a flash it was whipped away, curling in towards the hull of the wreck.

There was a cry of disappointment and immediately Charles Johnson swung the wheel of his boat to move in closer in an attempt to retrieve the line. It was a dangerous operation. Captain Grimstone jumped forward and, leaning over the end of the bridge, blew hard on his whistle to attract the coxswain's attention.

'Keep away!' he bawled through a megaphone, waving his arms to give emphasis to his warning. 'Keep away from the ship,' he repeated. 'It's too dangerous!'

'That was too risky,' said the captain to an officer. 'We can't have them taking chances like that, can we?'

It was an unselfish thing to do, but there is a code of behaviour among men who go down to the sea in ships that will not take safety for themselves at any cost. As William Hickson said later: 'For Coxswain Johnson to manoeuvre his boat in as he did with the tremendous sea that was running, and firing the line aboard to drop on the one and only place that we seamen could get it, and considering the force of the wind, was to us all a superb piece of seamanship.'

He added: 'But looking back, I think perhaps it was for the best that the line was not secured for I am quite sure that there would have been several fatal casualties and broken limbs in using the breeches-buoy across that gap where the waves were travelling at a tremendous height and force.'

At this time the *English Trader's* boilers were being wrenched from their beds and pushed into the sea. They presented a further hazard to the lifeboat when close to the wreck.

There was actually relief among the seamen when they saw Coxswain Johnson raise his hand in acknowledgement of the warning, and immediately put the wheel over to bring his boat away from the steamer. He, also, knew the risks were too great in that baffling, rising sea. The *Louise Stephens* swung off towards deep water. Once off the bank, the coxswain intended to anchor for the night if possible, or 'dodge' about using engines and the drogue to hold the *Louise Stephens* steady if necessary, to be on hand if conditions moderated. In any case, to renew rescue attempts in the morning when light came.

He moved over to *HMS Vesper* to tell her duty officer that he could not do any more at the moment, and of his intention to stay close by. But he was told through a loud-hailer that orders had been received for the boat to return at once. Charles Johnson was much annoyed for it meant the long haul back to Yarmouth in foul conditions and then to come out again in the morning. He was a strong-willed man and he got very 'hot under the collar', protesting forcibly that he was in a position to judge the best course. But the officer on the destroyer was merely acting in a liaison capacity and unable to change the instruction. The *Louise Stephens* had no alternative but to return to base.

The position of lifeboats coming under a measure of Naval control when going to sea made some friction. Some of it arose from the fact that, although the wooden lifeboats were not affected by magnetic mines which the Germans were laying by aircraft in close-coastal waters, particularly outside harbours, when they started to lay the acoustic mines it was not known whether the lifeboat's propellers were sufficient to detonate them. One of the Yarmouth-based torpedo boats was almost sunk by such a mine and while the uncertainty was there, the order was made that lifeboats must not put to sea without permission from the Naval duty officer. Moreover, although he could not order the lifeboat to go out, he could request it.

There is no doubt that the instruction was sound and in the best interests of the lifeboatmen as the Navy had information about enemy mine-laying activities and what channels had been swept, not known to the lifeboatmen. The situation regarding acoustic mines was eased at Yarmouth by the use of the rescue boat, *John and Mary Micklem,* which had a single engine and also a sail. Anything happening in Yarmouth Roads and she could be sailed out of harbour into the Cockle Gat and when clear of the danger area, start up her engine.

The failure of his five attempts was a bitter disappointment to Coxswain Johnson and his men. They had been so near – or seemed so near – to success. On the other hand, how they could have kept station against the wreck while her forty-four crew were transferred, and with the tide again building up, it is hard to visualise. It was of course, another blow to the men on the wreck. Yet the admiration they felt for the men in the little craft outweighed any despondency, and knowing what had happened to the *H F Bailey*, they expressed their concern about the Yarmouth lifeboat's attempts to rescue without the presence of another lifeboat to help if things went wrong. But they knew it would be a long time before the Cromer boat returned and although another lifeboat, perhaps Lowestoft, might be sent to their aid, they could not count on that. The Cromer crew had taken such a battering that she might not come back at all.

The end of daylight on that strange, stormy Sabbath was not far away. Already both sea and sky were taking on a darker hue. Nobody took much notice at the time as they were concerned with the operation to save them, until suddenly the destroyer was seen signalling to the *Louise Stephens* and the distorted sound of a voice calling through a loud-hailer, drifted gustily towards them.

The crew of the *Louise Stephens* could be seen through glasses making preparations as if to anchor, then she was observed to move closer to the *Vesper's* weather-side. Then the loud-hailer and lusty Norfolk voices could be heard fighting a duel. Most of the words were whipped away by the storm but the sailors on the wreck strained their ears trying to catch anything that would tell them the import of the exchange. They soon formed the conclusion, as much by the tone as by the words, that all was not harmony and the Yarmouth crew were angry and much displeased at some shore-based authority. Then the shouting and gesticulating ceased. The *Louise Stephens* moved astern, turning as she did so in a wide arc, and came within hailing distance of the *English Trader*. Before a gust of wind whipped the words away, the seamen caught: 'Don't worry, lads. We'll be back.'

Once again the raised arm waved farewell as the Yarmouth boat completed the turn and headed towards the distant Norfolk shore. She had over 20 miles to travel and it would soon be dark. She was, in fact, soon swallowed up in the dusk and by the intervening combers with their crests smoking white with spindrift.

There was of course, little alternative for the *Louise Stephens* but to return although she would have preferred to stay nearby in deep water and, had she ridden out the night, could have effected the rescue, but the crew of seven were 'knocked-up' after their many rescue attempts and to ride out this gale in a small boat through the autumn night would have been most exacting.

The sea had, in fact, won the second round also.

The seamen on the *English Trader* were perplexed by the argument between lifeboat and Naval vessel and did not know what would now happen. They wondered if the lifeboat had had a disagreement with the commander of the destroyer and in anger had called off the whole operation. Yet they knew that was most unlikely. If they had to go it was for some different and good reason. What was it? The answer came from the winking, shaded signalling lamp of the destroyer: 'Lifeboat has been ordered back to base. Owing to the adverse weather it would be dangerous for all concerned to carry on the rescue after dark.'

The signalman paused for a moment as if to let his message sink in, but in point of fact, he was probably receiving further instructions from the officer on watch. The lamp winked again: 'We shall be with you through the night. Please keep watch. Good luck.'

The message ended and the second mate acknowledged with a 'Thank you.'

Meanwhile, on the Cromer boat, now heading for Yarmouth helped by wind and tide, they made good speed even with the fouled propeller. They tried *en route,* to contact the Yarmouth Naval base by radio telephone, as they wanted a doctor to be at the quay to meet them, although they felt it would be too late.

It was a miserable journey. The signalman lay wrapped in blankets in the canopy and his comrades were doing what they could to revive him. But they could see their efforts were not going to avail. Halfway to Yarmouth, 'Boy Primo's' pulse ceased to beat. The signalman had died of heart failure.

They told Henry Blogg the news, but he already suspected it. A deep sense of grief weighed upon every man in this little tightly-knit fraternity. Whatever arguments, banter and occasionally jealousy there was, they were comrades. They had repeatedly faced dangers and arduous services together over many years and 'Boy Primo' was such a likeable, ready-to-help-anybody chap. It was the first death in the long and splendid history of the Cromer lifeboats, although one man had been crushed to death during a boat launching.

Edward Allen had served nearly forty years in the station's boats. He was popular and a good comrade. He was born at Cromer in 1892 and attended the local school on Louden Road until he was fourteen, and then he helped his father, Walter John or 'Catty' in the fishing boat. Both his grandfather Billy and his father had been lifeboatmen. It was a family tradition.

When 'Boy Primo' 'got a belt'* he had first borne the nickname 'Little Catty'.

*See Note 2, p 95.

Somehow this became 'Boy Primo'. No one knows why! But in small fishing communities, every son seems to take his father's Christian name and without nicknames it would be hard to distinguish whom one was speaking about. So most fishermen had a nickname – although Henry Blogg did not.

Edward Allen was connected with Cromer Wesleyan church all his life and was one of the society stewards. It was not uncommon when the maroons sounded over the town during a Sunday service to see him quietly pick up his cap, leave his seat and the church and dash for the boathouse. He was a staunch member of the local St John Ambulance Brigade. In fact, he had a reputation for his readiness to help in any good cause. His love of football made him active in the town reserve team as a young man and a keen supporter for the rest of his years.

In the First World War he enlisted in Kitchener's Army in 1914, in the Medical Corps. Later he joined the Royal Naval Reserve and was called up in 1918, serving on the *Normansk* minesweeper until June 1919. As a lifeboatman he was awarded a medal for his part in the *Fernebo* rescue in 1917.

During the Second World War, owing to bad weather, he was forced to come ashore in his fishing boat on the Runton side of Cromer and was promptly arrested and held in a local guardroom until he could be identified. This incident was a continual source of banter from his fellow fishermen – although they never knew when it might happen to them, for local fishermen had permits to use their own beach, but no other.

Edward Allen was one of the few men who has ever walked on the Haisborough Sands. Henry Blogg did so too and brought back some of the sand as a souvenir which his wife treasured and kept in a glass container. Edward dearly loved his pipe and when tobacco was in short supply in the war, he smoked tea – least his fellow fishermen said so – but tea was scarcer than tobacco!

A local magistrate recalls with a smile how 'Boy Primo' was in the ambulance one day when it was in collision with a private car. When the case came to court, 'Boy Primo' testified that the other car: 'appeared on our port-quarter and then ran athwart our bows.'

Henry Davies said of him: 'He was a good-living, lovable man. He gave all his leisure to the St John Ambulance and the lifeboat.'

It was a fitting tribute.

When the *H F Bailey* reached Yarmouth it was 6 pm. The dim lights of the boom appeared ahead and the tired crew took their boat through and made their way up the long channel to the Town Hall Quay. Waiting there was a doctor and ambulance as well as the police and other people connected with the lifeboat. The doctor confirmed that Edward Allen was dead. He also gave his attention to other members of the crew who had been washed overboard. Some of them were so affected by their ordeal that they had to be helped out of the boat.

Although Blogg was suffering from his experience, he insisted before he took food or rested, that his lifeboat must be ready to go out again, and he helped his mechanics refuel – a laborious business – carrying cans of fuel – and get her ready to return to the Knoll at first light. He was adamant about this because he knew he would then catch slack water on the bank. They did not try to clear the line wound round the propeller shaft as the boat was still in the water tied up at the quay. The crew were then taken to the Shipwrecked Sailors' Home where they were given hot baths, hot drinks, food and dry clothes. A telephone call was put through to Cromer asking for more clothes and a replacement for Edward Allen.

While these events were happening to the two lifeboats out in the North Sea, back at Cromer, the hours of that Sunday just dragged by. A sense of foreboding greater than the usual anxiety grew amongst the relatives of the crew. It was not merely the severity of the weather and the long distance the *H F Bailey* had to travel, but an inexplicable intuition of disaster.

Mrs Henry Davies who saw the boat launch at 8 am, stood on the windswept pier boards watching the spreading, white wake of the little craft as it fought its way eastward. After the boat was swallowed up in the haze of spray and rain, she returned, the waves crashing against the steel supports of the pier as she walked, and breaking in booming confusion on the beach. When at home she went about the usual household tasks but felt strangely disturbed. Her thoughts turned again and again to the sight of *H F Bailey* plunging into the storm – looking like a small beetle climbing the furrows of a ploughed field. Years later she was still unable to say why she was so worried on the mission. But at dinnertime, the sense of something being amiss grew until, when it was nearly half past two, a choking feeling came over her. She felt she could bear the waiting alone no longer. She left the house and her two children, and hurried to a neighbour, also the wife of a lifeboatman, saying: 'There is something wrong. I know there is.'

Her neighbour too, was anxious and the two women, clad in thick coats went out into the narrow windswept streets of the little town – where the fishermen's cottages huddle together as if for protection from the bullying, north-easterly winds – to see Mrs Ann Blogg living in Swallow Cottage. But Ann had no news. She had heard nothing since her husband left seven hours earlier. However, she telephoned the coastguard.

He could not tell them anything. There was nothing else to do but wait, wait, wait. The three women sat around a fire talking and speculating for an hour. Other women relatives of the crew also came seeking news of their menfolk. They too, stopped and waited until Ann telephoned the coastguard once more. This time he had just received a message – the Yarmouth base had taken a relayed message: 'Making for Yarmouth. Have ambulance ready at quay.'

The message itself did not unduly worry the women for it was not unusual. They thought the ambulance was needed for one of the men whom the crew rescued. So the group of women split up to return time and again for further news.

Soon after 6 pm the telephone in the hall rang and Ann, answering it, heard her husband speaking. His voice sounded husky and strained as he told her what had happened and how they had lost 'Boy Primo'. He said that a car would be leaving Cromer for Yarmouth with dry clothes for the crew and also bringing another signalman as a replacement for 'Boy Primo'. Ann went back to the other women who were still there and had heard some of the conversation. They knew there had been a disaster to their menfolk. She wept as she told them the message and their first thought was for someone to go and see Mrs Allen and break the grievous news to her. They then went home to get ready the clothes their men would need.

Later that evening a small fish-van picked up the clothes; boots, socks, underclothes and jerseys – ganseys, as Norfolk fishermen call their woollen jerseys – and George Cox went to take the place of the dead signalman.

Several hours later when the van had delivered the clothes at Yarmouth and picked up the wet gear of the Cromer crew, Mrs Henry Davies got a parcel of sodden garments. She was surprised to see her husband's watch, and more surprised to note that it had stopped at 2.28 – the very time he had been thrown into the water and the time she had experienced the overpowering foreboding of something being wrong.

Such things cannot be dismissed lightly as coincidence, nor can they be explained.

The crew of the *Louise Stephens* did not get back to Yarmouth until some four hours after the Cromer boat. They had a most difficult and perilous journey from the Knoll for with the gale and strong sea running, they had to make their way back to the coast mostly through thick darkness.

It was bright moonlight for brief periods and the lifeboatmen could see for miles. In fact, the sea had a silvery beauty despite its violence that has remained as an unfading memory with the *Louise Stephens'* mechanic ever since. When he recalls that hard trip back empty-handed from the Knoll, he says: 'I shall never forget how the sea looked when the moon broke through.'

When the almost-full moon shook off the shrouding clouds, the tumbling waters were like living silver. Tired as the lifeboatmen were, it impressed them. But when the clouds closed in the ensuing darkness seemed more thick. Out of the shipping channel there were no buoys to guide them. As they neared the coast, the beauty of the wild wind-blown sky and brief moments of light were lost and they almost groped their way, for there was little means of telling where they were. Then the helmsman saw a dull light in the dark distance. It stayed a second or two then went out. It re-appeared. They knew it was Winterton Coastguard Station. Samuel Halfnight had, at one time, been signalman in the Yarmouth boat. He joined the Coastguard Service and was on duty that night at Winterton Station. He had of course, been informed that the *Louise Stephens* was on her way back from the sandbank and he saw her navigation light through his telescope. Appreciating the difficulties they were facing, he gave them the guidance of a dull light. It enabled Coxswain Johnson to get a bead on the light and come south to the North Cockle and North Scroby.

It was here that the lifeboat got the force of the NNE gale as a free or tail wind, and the danger of an over-running sea was real. At times a wave overtook, slid under the keel and ran ahead of the boat. Once with the moon reappearing, one of the crew saw a large following wave bearing down upon them. He yelled: 'Look out – here's a big one!'

Fortunately it went under the lifeboat lifting her high like a cork and carrying her forward as it went. Then it ran on. The lifeboat slipped back into the succeeding trough. Had that sea broken on them it would have buried them by the immense weight of water.

Keeping as near inshore as he dare, Charles Johnson was able at times to pick out the silhouette of a landmark which served him as a guide until he made harbour. He discerned the faint lights of the boom. It was opened and he too, like the Cromer coxswain, tied up. It was then 10.30 pm. They used their own jetty and climbed up the steps after one of the most exhausting and demanding journeys any of the crew had ever known.

It was inky darkness as they tied up at the dreary jetty with the sea, even in the harbour, tossing and throwing their boat about. The wind was banging and rattling tins, timbers and anything loose. Salt had inflamed their eyes; their faces and hair ran with sea-water; they were so wet and cold Coxswain Johnson decided he would leave the task of refuelling until the morning. Before his crew were taken or made their own way to their homes, he told them to reassemble at 5.30 am. He was determined to go back and complete the job that they had so nearly accomplished. So they went to their homes, utterly weary, the skin on their faces stiffening as the salt dried. In the mind of each man however, was the fear that during the hours of the night, if the gale and heavy seas kept up, the *English Trader* might be broken up and the remaining 44 men on her lost. But there was nothing else they could do.

That night at the Shipwrecked Sailors' Home, Henry Blogg did not rest his salt-stung eyes or go to bed until he knew that the *Louise Stephens* had berthed and after giving Charles Johnson time to get to his home, he telephoned him. The two coxswains discussed arrangements for the next day and the renewed attempt to get the shipwrecked men off.

Blogg said he wanted to get out as early as he could to take advantage of the tide gap on the Knoll which gave them their best chance of a rescue.

Johnson told Blogg of his five attempts to get to the wreck and how they had actually moored until the rope parted. Henry Blogg told his fellow coxswain that any boat which got alongside that ship in the conditions then prevailing on the bank had accomplished a fine feat of seamanship. He said that he was going to try at 4 am but Johnson said he would wait for daylight.

The rules governing the boom were that it would be closed from sun-down to sun-up, and the Flag Officer-in-Charge of the base had told Henry Blogg that his boat was not to leave without his permission.

CHAPTER 8
Another Night on the Wreck

 WITH ALL this activity on shore at Cromer and Yarmouth among the lifeboat folk, away in the North Sea the drama had still to be played out through the hours of darkness. So far, the sea had been swaggeringly triumphant – but all was not finished.

On board the wreck, the men knew they must try to survive till dawn whatever the night might bring. There was no hope of rescue or help from the destroyer. They must hope the lifeboats would return with the new day. Still, it was a comfort to know *HMS Vesper* was there – the sea did not look quite so empty!

It is an indication of the gale's ferocity that Convoy EC90 which had steamed on up the East Coast to the Firth of Forth, was twelve hours late arriving at its Scottish destination.

Throughout the night the sea kept up its battering and display of ill-temper. The men in the chartroom felt at times caged up, almost like rats caught in a trap; on all sides peril surrounded that small room. After the *Louise Stephens* left the Knoll at 6.30 pm, the flood-tide came and the seas worsened. The whine of the gale in the rigging rose at times to a shrill whistle or it made deep moaning sounds around parts of the superstructure. For some periods during the first part of the night, the near-full moon broke through its cloud-shield to shed a pallid almost ghostly light on the scene. It not only showed up the wind-torn masses of dark cloud, but it had an eerie quality, making the big seas seem bigger and the torn jagged edges of the ship's upperworks take fantastic shapes. When the light fell on the seas as they raced onwards to the wreck and then spilled over her, often flooding the entire length, it gave them a beauty that made them fascinating, yet frightening. The spindrift and flying spray when the seas hit the ship seemed silvery and also phosphorescent. The white tops of breaking waves shone clear and silvery.

At some time during the night of harrowing waiting, a heavy sea broke the starboard wing of the bridge, tearing it completely away. William Hickson said: 'It sounded like the collapse of the Forth Bridge.'

It ripped the structure loose and left it hanging over the fore-deck, a mass of twisted metal and splintered wood. There it stayed, swaying back and forth, its creaking and groaning added to the babel of the elements as they played with it. Even more disturbing were the ominous rumbles which echoed up from below as parts of the ship collapsed. Bulkheads gave way. The two single-ended boilers had been lifted right out of their beds and washed out of the ship to the accompaniment of alarming structural banging. These noises deep in the bowels of the steamer could not be located but were often followed by sudden shockwaves passing through the decks. These heavy vibrations certainly made every man, from the captain downwards, uneasy. The more experienced of the crew felt the more alarmed, as it suggested the breaking up of the entire ship. When the moon shone they could see the gaping crack across the fore-deck where the ship had broken her back. It had widened appreciably. If the ship split into two parts the seas would probably reach them in the chartroom. There would be no refuge. At the moment their shelter was intact but the rampaging seas could alter that.

By 7 pm that Sunday night most of the seamen were trying to make themselves as comfortable as they could in the chartroom as it was the highest part of the superstructure, except the Monkey Island above it – and that was quite open to wind and sea. The chartroom measured about twelve feet by eight feet. The chart drawers were pulled out and used to sit on. A small settee and upturned buckets made seats as did the tabletop and shelves pulled out of the flag locker. Probably the best find for the men was the flags in the locker. These were quickly put to use as wrappings round wet shoulders, cushions and substitute towels.

The captain was amused when it was pointed out to him that the flag he had wrapped about his shoulders was, in fact, the quarantine flag. Stuck out there in the dark North Sea with no one able to get near them was like a quarantine!

Earlier, Captain Grimstone had taken off his own greatcoat and wrapped it about an injured fireman when the captain found him shivering violently with the cold. So quarantine or not, he was glad of the additional warmth from the dreaded flag.

To lessen the darkness and gloom in the chartroom each man in turn and at intervals – for a long night still lay ahead of them – would switch on his lifejacket lamp. This gave out a bright yellow glow, sufficient to see the full length of the room. It made the place a little less eerie. It was also some comfort to see one's shipmates. At this time the steward's forethought in getting all the cigarettes he could carry from the pantry was most appreciated. At times, the atmosphere in the crowded room became a little blue with cigarette smoke, but the gale soon took care of this by sucking it out through the open doorway like a suction fan. This door had been secured in the open position as a precaution lest it should become jammed and imprison the men inside. The chartroom had no other way out that could be used and it might become necessary to make a hurried exit – where to was another matter!

It was through the chartroom doorway that a watch was kept on the *HMS Vesper*. There was consolation in seeing the dim shape rise and fall with the combers although of course, there were no lights showing or signs of activity. But the destroyer's watch-keepers were maintaining their vigil.

The hours dragged by, but not in boredom for too much was at stake for the men to be bored. William Hickson had taken all but one of the shelves out of the flag locker – the flags had already been removed and put to good use -- and squeezed himself into it. It was not wide enough for him to move his arms once he was inside, but he could move his forearms up and down and use his hands. The bottom shelf made a useful seat. When his nearest shipmate, the steward, sitting on an upturned bucket, lit a cigarette for him he could get it to his mouth and enjoy it. Despite the discomfort of his cramped quarters he was glad to be in the locker. Although he felt like a sardine in a tin, it was warmer than in the rest of the room.

The two injured firemen were in some pain. They had been given aspirins and what first-aid could be rendered and were laid under the table to get as much space and shelter as possible. Apart from the captain's greatcoat, flags were tucked round them. One of the men began repeating the words of the Lord's Prayer. Over and over again in a weak, scarcely audible voice he said the words that have sustained so many in times of crisis and suffering.

Captain Grimstone listened and suggested they should all join in. The 44 shipwrecked men, accompanied – or mocked by – hostile sounds of wind and sea, said together the familiar words. The sudden and brutal fate of their shipmates, broken and thrown overboard, was in many minds. When the prayer ended the captain reminded them that it was Sunday night and that folk on shore would be, or had been in church and would be thinking of them. 'They will know we are here,' he said, 'and their prayers will be for us.'

Did beleaguered seamen only turn to prayer when other help failed and everything looked mighty unstable? Was it a last resort?

William Hickson says it was not. Although a merchant seaman's life is hard and tough, particularly in the early years of World War II, the gun layer met many deeply religious sailors in his years at sea, and when the ship was in port, several of the crew would make their way to the Mission for Seamen, for a service. The visit of the Padre was almost always welcome to the men although much depended on the character of the Padre. In the chartroom that night, there was no difficulty for the seamen to remember and repeat the Lord's Prayer.

And later when one of the firemen was having a bout of pain and foreboding about seeing daylight again, William Hickson heard one of the crew talking to him in a low voice saying: 'Put your hand in Mine,' said the Lord, 'and I will lead you through the darkness.' The words may have been mis-quoted by the seaman, but they helped the injured comrade.

At around midnight there was a heavy, distinctly metallic thumping on the weather-side of the hull below the bridge. It continued for a time at irregular intervals and was most noticeable when a particularly heavy sea came aboard. The thought uppermost in everyone's mind was that this was another mine, so they stopped talking or even moving and listened apprehensively. If is was a mine there was nothing they could do to fend it off. As a precaution, the captain ordered the men sitting near the starboard door to move away from it.

Presently the bumping stopped and they concluded and hoped for their own peace of mind, that whatever it was had been washed away from the wreck. It might have been another mine. It is unlikely it was a barrel from the cargo. They never knew but were not sorry it did not return.

At long intervals, *HMS Vesper* used a searchlight or sent up a flare to check that the situation had not worsened appreciably on the wreck. The sight of the vivid light illuminating the spot was cheering. It made them feel less isolated. Cooped up they were, but not forsaken. Even though stranded on a sea-beleaguered sandbank, they had company!

The banging and thumping in the ship did not diminish as time passed. If anything, the hammering and grinding became more disconcerting, with tearing, creaks, groans and strange vibrations that told them how the vessel was settling lower in the sand as well as being torn apart. It was like being in a broker's yard – only the sea was the scrap merchant.

What many of the men in the chartroom did not know was that a wing of the bridge had entirely collapsed and if anyone had forced open the other door in the room and gone out, he would have dropped 30 feet into the sea. Those who knew this had happened did not talk about it but kept the sobering knowledge to themselves. Needless to say, Captain Grimstone had ensured that the door was locked and no one could go through it without his knowing.

There was no food or drink of any kind but the cigarettes were more than welcome. Each man had his own supply and the glow of burning ends or the flare of a struck match in the gloom, when no lifejacket light was burning, was pleasant. No one bothered about the ill effects of chain-smoking that night!

William Hickson, cramped as he was in the flag locker, recalls that in spite of his discomfort, he dozed off from time to time. He had been up since 6 am on Saturday morning – over forty hours before – and had been on the gun-deck and busy all the time. He had been drenched repeatedly and, like most of his comrades, had spells of violent shivering. Nevertheless, Nature is a demanding lady and his fatigue and the draught-free locker made him doze off. Then, after he had nodded off, something extra loud would sound in the ship and wake him.

He began talking to the steward next to him who lit several cigarettes for him. In subdued voices they recalled earlier times of crisis. William Hickson found himself turning his thoughts again and again to his days as an apprentice on the *Warspite* – his longing for a sea life had brought him into many tight situations, but none as tight as this.

At times the two men thought of home and wondered what their relatives had been doing that day while they had been under the sea's mauling. They also speculated on just how the ship had struck and what was her likelihood of staying together till the lifeboats returned. They agreed she had driven hard onto the sand and was settling deeper every hour due to her own weight and the scouring action of the waves. This would be particularly severe under the bows where her hull had less draught. Amidships and aft where the hull had greater draught, the steamer was buried deep in the sand. They also commented that the sole remaining raft on the fore-deck had been torn loose and raked overboard, so there was now neither raft nor serviceable lifeboat left on board.

For most of the men in the chartroom, the hours crawled by, but some managed to sleep a little and fitfully. Subconsciously the uproar of the storm was still there. The steward, sitting on an upturned bucket against the flag locker and using a folded flag as a cushion, leaned his back against the frame of the locker and lit cigarette after cigarette. He frequently complimented himself that he had had the foresight to provide that single comfort.

The third mate had checked that the early morning full flood tide would be at about 6 am. Wondering how much the ship had settled in the sand and how much the tide would flow, many wondered if the high tide might reach the bridge. If so, the waves would swamp the whole structure including the chartroom. It would be pitch dark at that hour. Later on, men talked over their thoughts and fears, and this one was uppermost in many minds as the hour of six drew near.

If the tide was full, conversation was at a low ebb. Those who still felt like talking did so in low tones. Now and again there was a stir as one of the men eased an aching body. Several times the whole deck moved or shuddered violently as a particularly vicious sea hit it.

At some time after 5 am and certainly before 6 o'clock, the thunder of the giant waves seemed more pronounced, much heavier as they pounded the *English Trader*. When this happened, conversation ceased altogether. Men were listening. Those who were dozing seemed to realise the change, and opening their eyes they also listened. No one yet knew what was happening, but something was different and the roar of the sea seemed much greater. The men looked at one another in the feeble light of a nearly worn-out torch lying on the table. A big comber shook the ship as it thundered across the broken fore-deck. Spray rattled like hail against the steel shutters of the wheelhouse. Another was followed. It sounded farther off and broke over the fo'c'sle head, hissing and rumbling and then died away.

There was no mistaking now what had happened and the sailors listened, hardly believing they heard aright. The seconds ticked away before anyone dared to speak then Captain Grimstone said, in a quiet voice but one filled with emotion: 'Thank God, the wind's dropped.'

A sigh of relief and a few muttered words went up from the miserably wet and hungry men. They were the best words they had heard for many a day.

CHAPTER 9
Rescued

 THE THIRD round of this fight with the North Sea began at 3.30 am on Monday morning in Yarmouth. Henry Blogg was up and had already obtained weather reports from the Naval base and from Cromer coastguard. Both reports agreed that there was an improvement, but that: ' . . . it was nothing to write home about.'

The wind had eased slightly and the seas were not so heavy. In the cold and dark of the deserted, blacked-out quay, the *H F Bailey* crew assembled. Some were still heavy-eyed; some were unshaven and the driving wind and lashing salt spray of yesterday had reddened their faces. They looked tired and they were. One does not lightly shake off the pummelling they had endured for so long the previous day.

They also looked sober and grim-faced. There was none of the usual banter, but each man had an air of resolution. They were in no mood to chat. Several of these crewmen had raced to the Cromer boathouse to 'grab a belt' when the call came on Sunday morning – for there was still competition among the young men not yet called to the Forces – to man the lifeboat. What they had faced on the Knoll was part of a job they knew carried risks and they did not grouse now when their coxswain called them out of bed after such a brief rest. The same resolve was shown by each of the dozen men – to see this job through. They had come back last night with a dead comrade and the men they had set out to save were still stuck out in the North Sea on a disintegrating wreck. They wanted to ensure that there was something to put on the 'credit' side of this service. So hardly a word was spoken other than a command as they took their stations in the *H F Bailey*, cast off from the rain-drenched quay and slipped over the dark, troubled water to the harbour mouth.

It was 4.15 am. Most of the folk of Yarmouth and Gorleston were fast asleep on the chill Monday morning when Henry Blogg asked the Naval duty officer of the base to arrange for the boom to be opened to let them out. He did not ask permission nor did he inform the Flag Officer of his intending departure, but he probably stressed to the duty officer the need to get to the Knoll at the time of slack water. Possibly he looked askance at anything that merely savoured of red tape when lives were at stake. He must have realised that the security of the harbour rested with the Flag Officer, and what had happened at Scapa Flow in 1939 when a U-boat penetrated the harbour and destroyed a battleship had been a warning to all officers responsible for coastal havens.

Henry Blogg did, however, try to contact Charles Johnson by telephone to tell him he was now going out to the sandbank, but he could not get through to the Yarmouth coxswain. So he asked the telephone operator to give him a message as soon as he could.

The little touch of courtesy to another coxswain, and the 'blind eye' to the Flag Officer's orders were typical of Henry Blogg. It was another 'Nelson touch'. This son of Cromer, bred in the ways of the sea from boyhood, possessed that quality of daring and perseverance, combined with consummate seamanship, which wanted to get on with an urgent job and chafed at a petty restriction.

At 4.40 am, the 65-year-old coxswain, who had been washed from his boat some 14 hours earlier into bitterly cold seas, and had battled for ten hours with gale-lashed waters, having had little or no sleep since, was passing through the harbour boom and into the Roads. He was hoarse from having to shout his orders yesterday against the noise of the sea. He had three hours of darkness ahead of him and rough seas and was less familiar with these waters than his own area about Cromer. The rope was still around the propeller shaft so that one engine was not giving full power. There was also the emotional distress of having lost a comrade and memories that went too deep for speech. The crew could not yet talk about 'Boy Primo'.

As the lifeboat pulsed north-eastward, scarcely a word was uttered. The churned, white wake of the boat spreading, but swiftly lost in the heaving seas, marked their passage, and the wet oilies of the crew shone in the deck-lights. They had steamed through the Barley Picle and Cockle Gat, getting as much protection as they could from the wind and spray. But as they turned eastward to pass the South Haisbro', conditions improved; the wind that had buffetted them for so long veered to the north-west and eased greatly. It seemed to them as if the weather, relenting of its hostility and brutality, had changed both mind and heart, for soon the seas also moderated and the prospects of getting the shipwrecked men off were good.

Three hours and twenty minutes after leaving Yarmouth – exactly 24 hours after they had set out from Cromer on this service, they neared Hammond Knoll. Through the haze of spray and spindrift they saw first the destroyer still keeping vigil and then the *English Trader*. All eyes except the mechanics searched the decks for signs of life. Soon figures could be distinguished moving, and then arms waving. The sound of a faint cheer came to them over the water. There was relief on the *H F Bailey* that the crew had survived the long wild night on the sands.

On the wreck itself, soon after 7 am, the grey, reluctant daylight had spread across sky and wave-top. The outlines of the *English Trader* began to fill in with detail as the light strengthened. John Elliott, standing in the doorway of the chartroom, had been staring for long periods over the waters as the autumn light strengthened. Then he half-turned to Captain Grimstone and quietly said: 'It's now like a mill-pond out there sir.'

The statement was of course, an exaggeration, but after the tumbling, crazy seas they had endured for 48 hours, it was an excusable over-statement. Anyway, as man after man hurriedly got up from his cramped position and threaded his way through the tangle of limbs and bodies of his shipmates to see the change for himself, there was no disputing that the sea was a sane and sober creature compared with the insensate, furious animal that had raged on the Knoll a few hours earlier. No one dared read too much into the change. It was an unspeakable relief to see it but it could be only a temporary lull. Such is often the case in this area of the North Sea. However, the wind was veering to the north-west and that was a good sign. They took heart and cheered one another with a joke and laugh at the easing of the weather. Then a couple of strong gusts broke the comparative calm of the wind – and laughed back at them. The gale could start another blow yet and there was still no sign of lifeboats.

Moreover, looking towards the *HMS Vesper*, they were reminded that their troubles were not over for they still had another enemy. With the coming of daylight there was the possibility, indeed the probability that German aircraft would be on the prowl. If so, held fast on the bank, they offered a plum target. An attack by a Dornier would leave them unable to take avoiding action and unable to fire back for their guns were either under water or unreachable. However, across a few hundred yards of water, they had a guardian – *HMS Vesper*, and she had teeth! From the wreck they could see details of her various pieces of armament and knew the guncrews were at their stations. The shipwrecked men did not feel so helpless and naked should an attack develop.

Strangely, even as they were discussing this, they heard the drone of aircraft and peered anxiously through the door as the sound came rapidly closer. The planes were approaching fast and there was immediate relief when they recognised the familiar note of single-engined Spitfires. Two fighter planes, probably from RAF Station Coltishall, circled the ship and dipped their wings in answer to the sailors waving from the bridge of the wreck. They then flew westward.

Scarcely ten minutes had passed after the aircraft left when the destroyer lamp winked a cheering message: 'Lifeboats are on the way.'

It had just gone 8 am when the Cromer boat was sighted. She was sending up a shower of spray as she plunged at maximum speed considering her fouled propeller, through the seas. Forty-two men, unshaven, bleary-eyed and very tired, stood about the bridge, easing their stiff limbs from long hours in confined positions and silently watched the plume of spray. As the lifeboat neared it looked like a white moustache at the bows.

The sea that had snarled and clawed at them for nearly two days was now almost docile. Sand-stained waves still surged across the wreck but Henry Blogg could see as he got within a couple of hundred yards that it would be possible to get right alongside on the lee-side. He gave orders to be ready fore and aft with fenders, boathooks and lines. There was no need this time to circle and survey the best method of approach.

'Thank God,' he said as he steamed determinedly in to the *English Trader*. 'We'll have 'em off there this morning, lads.'

The engines were throttled back and the *H F Bailey* brought slowly into a position opposite the bridge of the wreck. Blogg was watching the jagged projections of broken plate and girders, but there were no floating objects to avoid near the wreck. The derricks were no danger. The oilies and sou'westers of the Cromer men gleamed, making them resemble an advertisement for tinned fish as they stood, boathooks, fenders and lines ready to grapple and hold. Then an order was shouted and the hooks caught the twisted rails of the wreck. The deck of the steamer had so settled in the sand that it was but two feet higher than that of the *H F Bailey*. The fenders were dropped. Mooring ropes were made fast fore and aft. It was but a little jump to the lifeboat deck.

Captain Grimstone gave his last order from the bridge: 'Abandon ship!'

The seamen left their ship. Helped by the lifeboatmen, they jumped or dropped onto the heaving deck of the *H F Bailey*. The two injured seamen were assisted from the chartroom and into the rescuing craft as she bumped and rolled against the hull of the steamer.

'It's a piece of cake this morning,' said Henry Blogg to Jack Davies.

On the wreck, Captain Grimstone stood watching his men clamber from the doomed vessel. Then he made a gesture towards the lifeboat and said to William Hickson: 'All right, Gunner, you can go now. The captain always goes last, you know!'

As he too dropped on to the *H F Bailey* deck, the ropes were cleared and boathooks freed. The survivors made their way round the lifeboat, getting shelter where they could or standing at the rails as the two engines came to life and the boat with her load of 56 men churned away from the freighter. The whole operation had taken but 30 minutes and had been as Blogg said: 'A piece of cake.'

The injured men were put into the cabin's shelter and given tots of rum and what aid was possible. Biscuits were handed round to the hungry seamen. Captain Grimstone, the officers and some of the men looked back from the heaving deck of the saving craft to the *English Trader* as she was left to her fate

Opposite, the Cromer lifeboat, the H.F. Bailey *approaching the* English Trader *early on Monday morning, when the seas had somewhat abated, to make the rescue of the crew. This picture was taken from the freighter by the 4th Engineer.*

Above, top left: Cromer cox'n Henry Blogg. Top right: Gun layer William Hickson. Below left: George Mobbs, Yarmouth and Gorleston lifeboat mechanic in 1941. Below right: Henry 'Shrimp' Davies of the Cromer lifeboat talking to Robert Cross of the Humber lifeboat on Spurn Point in the 1960's.

Opposite, the Cromer lifeboat crew, photographed after a mission in 1939. Left to right: G. Cox, R. Cox, J.R. Davies, J.J. Davies Jnr., W.H. Davies, J.J. Davies Snr., H. Blogg, J.W. Davies, H.T. 'Shrimp' Davies, F. Davies, R.C. Davies, W.H. Davies.

To illustrate conditions at sea – Yarmouth and Gorleston lifeboat leaving harbour

The H.F. Bailey *launching at Cromer.*

– a sorry, broken wreck. For most of the crew she meant little, they had only just joined, but to those who had sailed many thousands of miles in her, got used to her rolling whims and tantrums, there was a sense of loss. She had been their home – their ship. Perhaps some of them felt even the sea was on the side of the enemy! But it was not so. The sea was quite neutral, caring no more for the Germans than the British. Of the 4,786 Allied vessels sent to the bottom between 1939 and 1945, only 8% were from marine causes. U-boats and mines accounted for 69%; air attacks for 16% and surface ships for 7%.

The *English Trader* was part of the 8%!

When the *H F Bailey* turned from the casualty, *HMS Vesper* signalled the coxswain: 'Are you bringing the survivors on board?'

Standing at the helm, Blogg repeated the signal to himself as it was given to him and turning to the greyfaced, bedraggled survivors about him, asked: 'Do you want to go aboard the destroyer? We have everything waiting for you ashore, and they'll be expecting you.'

William Hickson stood near the coxswain as he spoke and he recalls that as the weather-beaten face of Cromer's skipper ranged over the tired faces of the seamen he had rescued at such cost to himself and his men, tears trickled down his face. It was not the effect of the wind which had eased, nor was it the North Sea spray. Much of his emotion welled from the knowledge that 'Boy Primo' had died, but had not given his life vainly.

The seamen looked at Henry Blogg. They had never seen him before in their lives, but stranger though he was, he had risked his own and his crew's lives to rescue them. They gave the answer he expected. 'We are coming with you,' they said. 'You rescued us. We'll stay here with you.'

'I thought you would say that,' answered Henry and a smile wreathed his face. He turned to his mechanic: 'Tell them, Billy, the men will stay with us.'

Then he called out as the message ended: 'Full speed ahead.' And the splendid boat seemed to roar her eagerness to get back to harbour and complete a good job.

The escort destroyer which had stood so faithfully by the stricken *English Trader*, unable to get her crew off but giving them comfort through the night's vigil, weighed anchor and returned to Sheerness. Nursing the straggler in trouble had been a tedious but necessary job.

In daylight, with the wind and sea much more friendly, the *H F Bailey* covered the distance to Yarmouth in good time despite her handicap of increased weight and the impaired propeller. But to the survivors who had no duty to perform, it seemed a long, long journey to the shore. They could move about the deck and exercise their limbs and keep circulation moving, but they were hungry, longing for a steaming mug of tea which was not available on the lifeboat – and very tired.

After three hours of good running, the boom was winched open and the *H F*

Bailey, it seemed rather proudly with her crowded deck, steamed up to the Town Hall Quay, arriving at 11.30 am. The survivors saw a group of folk waiting for them with an ambulance. But this was not needed. The boat tied up and the seamen were helped up the steps onto the quay. Ready hands offered to help William Hickson, but he said cheerily: 'I don't need any help, but thank you.'

A motor coach moved forward to the men and the 44 climbed into it and were driven away to the Shipwrecked Sailors' Home. There they were given that long-anticipated steaming mug of tea, the sight of a blazing fire and the knowledge that already a hot meal was nearly ready. After hot baths and a change of clothes where possible, the men sat down to the first meal for over 40 hours. They were not long before they went to their rooms and climbed into beds with warm blankets, seeking in sleep to forget some of the fears and horror they had known on Hammond Knoll.

Meanwhile the Cromer boat was berthed next to the Gorleston lifeboathouse as she could not yet return to her own shed at Cromer. The seas were still running too high. The 12 Cromer men were taken home by car and some returned the next day to bring back that stable, splendid-looking boat, the *H F Bailey*, to a well-earned rest in her shed at the end of the pier.

When the *H F Bailey* had tied up at Yarmouth and unloaded her precious cargo of seamen, the *Louise Stephens* was still well out in the North Sea. At 6.30 am that morning, she had loosed her moorings and, with the boom opened, steamed for Hammond Knoll. Her crew, of course, found conditions so mitigated that they made the journey in less than three hours. When they reached the sandbank they saw the dark shape of the casualty, but the destroyer had gone. They rightly assumed the rescue had been effected. However, they moved in closer without difficulty and saw the decks awash and the bridge was deserted. Their journey was abortive. But the Yarmouth men had done their duty.

The *Louise Stephens* turned about and steamed back to her base, re-entering the harbour at 11.50am – not long after the Cromer boat had moored at the Town Hall Quay.

The Cromer crew heard later from a vessel in the Knoll vicinity the next day that the *English Trader* had gone completely under the water. The sands had swallowed her – claiming yet another valuable ship and a million pound cargo. Nevertheless, the third and decisive round of that East Coast combat had been won by the lifeboats!

On Tuesday, 28th October, the seamen went to their homes or, in the case of William Hickson, to London to report to *HMS President.* There he was given 21 days' survivor's leave. Not surprisingly he had developed a really heavy cold that he could not shake off for a very long time. But otherwise physically he was none the worse for his grim experiences on the bank.

For this fine service, the RNLI made the following awards: Henry Blogg was awarded the third clasp to the Institution's silver medal. The rest of the crew were awarded either the bronze medal or a clasp. They also received the thanks of the Institution on vellum. Edward Allen's widow received a relative's certificate recording the gallantry of his death and a pension as though he had been killed in action.

George Cox, who took the place of the signalman, also received the Institution's thanks on vellum.

The RNLI awarded Coxswain Charles Johnson the bronze medal for his determination and seamanship in getting a line aboard in the seas then running. The other six members of the Yarmouth boat were awarded the Institution's thanks on vellum.

Being wartime, the rescue could receive little publicity, but messages of congratulation came from many quarters, including the Flag Officer of the Naval base and from the ship's owners. Expressions of sympathy also poured in to Mrs Allen.

Henry Blogg retired as coxswain in 1947, and was aptly titled the 'Greatest of the Lifeboatmen'. During his 53 years as a lifeboatman, the Cromer boats had gone out on 387 missions and rescued 873 lives. No other lifeboatman has received so many decorations for gallantry. Apart from three gold medals, he won four silver medals. He also held the George Cross and the British Empire Medal. He died in July 1954 aged 78 years. Both the Italian and French governments awarded Henry Blogg medals for services to their national ships.

The mission to the *English Trader* had been his toughest test.

Epilogue

 ALMOST AS a postscript to this story of the loss of the *English Trader* comes the realisation that this grim weekend ordeal for the seamen and their rescue by Britain's lifeboat crews was but a chapter in the sea-going story of William Hickson. It was another incident, packed with drama, peril and sorrow, in the eventful life of a lad who yearned to go to sea and made his career in the Navy. It is to men like him who kept open the sea lanes of this island during two world wars, when the threat of starvation was most real, that we owe such a heavy debt of gratitude. So often they had to take persistent punishment from the sea and also from the enemy without being able to strike back.

After his survivor's leave, marred by a streaming cold, William Hickson returned and again reported to *HMS President*. He was signed on a small ship plying between the Tyne and London carrying coal to power stations. This suited him well for, after two years of cross-Atlantic voyages he had seen little of his family and now he could get home frequently, if only for days at a time.

Before he went aboard his new ship he was delighted to see Dan and Jacko, two of his gunners from the *English Trader*. They too were awaiting a ship. The three men hoped to be allotted to the same vessel to renew their comradeship. In fact, William Hickson made a point of asking the Master-at-arms: 'Can these two men be drafted with me?'

'I am afraid not,' was the answer.

'We've sailed together a long time. I'd very much like to have them with me.'

'Sorry, but you know what regulations are. They're allotted elsewhere.'

So regretfully the three men went separate ways and have never seen each other again.

After a period on this small coastal vessel, William Hickson was detailed to a ship which was being fitted out as an ammunition carrier. He did not relish the idea at all!

Who would?

When she was ready, he joined her and sailed to the Mediterranean. There for nearly two years with seamen-gunners as his staff, he encountered so many hazards that even now he wonders how he survived. There were attacks from German and Italian aircraft and submarines; E-boats – not to mention mines, magnetic, acoustic and just plain-flavoured! In that time he had crowded in enough adventure to last a lifetime. He longed for something less noisy, less demanding and more secure.

Now, from the comparative haven of retirement, he looks back on those turbulent years, very occasionally turning out old photographs of ships and shipmates, and souvenirs of '. . . old unhappy far-off days and battles long ago.'

And he looks back on his early years. Born at Petham near Canterbury, William Hickson's early years were full of change, for his father, a naval man, was killed soon after William was born and the heavy responsibility of bringing up him and his two sisters fell upon his mother. He therefore, spent much time with relatives or foster parents. His love of the sea was inborn, for two uncles as well as his father, had been in the Navy. When 13 years old, he yearned to go to sea, so his mother made enquiries and helped by the fact that his father had been in the Navy, he was accepted for a two-year apprenticeship in the Training Ship *Warspite*. When he was 14 he left school at Waltham and went to Greenhithe in Kent, where the *Warspite* was anchored in the Thames. She had been a light cruiser, *HMS Hermione* and saw action at the battle of Jutland. She is now stationed in the River Medway. William remembers that he was indeed following in his father's footsteps for his father had been on this self-same ship when she was in action. Young William Hickson found discipline on the *Warspite* strict and the life tough. He loved and had grown up to a country life, and the ship seemed almost a prison. Looking back now on his training he admits how efficient it was.

One clause of his apprenticeship was that if he proved efficient he could go to sea in a merchant ship and thus obtain real sailing experience; the aim of the training ship being to train boys of good character for the Merchant Navy as well as the Royal Navy.

So, after 15 months on the *Warspite,* having proved himself proficient, William Hickson was sent to Cardiff and signed on as a deck boy on the *SS Miguel de Larrinaga,* a freighter registered in Liverpool, owned by the Larrinaga Company. She carried a cosmopolitan crew of Malays, Spaniards, Negroes and Irishmen. Mostly her officers were British. The 15-year-old lad, however, got on well with all members of this mixed crew. The bo'sun, a gigantic Malay who had been a pearl-diver, took an almost fatherly interest in him and kept him at his studies, constantly impressing upon him the necessity of getting his second mate's ticket.

One incident he has never forgotten; one day he was taken to the bridge to be shown how the ship steered. After some time he was allowed to take over the helm, with the second officer watching him. He felt immensely proud and important steering the big ship on her course and was getting along fine. After a time, the officer moved away from him and leaned casually over the rails gazing across the sea. The young man, thinking that he was doing so well that the wheel was being left to him, grew over-confident. Suddenly the officer straightened up and leapt to the helm.

'Look what you are doing, young man,' he cried. The ship was getting off course. William Hickson wondered how the officer knew but later realised that while leaning on the rails, the man appearing so casual was in reality carefully watching the wake of the vessel and saw her deviation in course.

After nine months, William Hickson left, much to the mate's annoyance, and signed on the *SS Indian Transport,* registered in London. He found life aboard her hard. She had no electric light, oil lamps being used; and the decks were so loaded with cargo that it was usually difficult to get about the ship. After six months on her he was glad to move to the *SS Pencarrow,* registered in Falmouth. After two or three voyages in this ship, Hickson signed on the *SS Pilar de Larrinaga,* sister ship to the *Miguel.*

So, seven years of seafaring, meeting all kinds of men, learning all kinds of things and visiting far places, passed and William Hickson grew tired of the life at sea. He wanted a settled job ashore, and although he was seeing some of the famed cities of the world, there were long periods of utter boredom. He became restless in mind and unsettled.

Things came to a head one day when talking with an old Norwegian sailor. Leaning on the rails, looking at the wide circle of a flat sea, chatting and smoking, they got talking about the future and the older man said: 'You've got to make up your mind soon, young fellow, if this is the life you want. Look at it,' he indicated the sea, 'rolling there incessantly empty, anonymous, drear. I'm an old man now and I've been doing just that all my years. Looking out over grey water day after day and I'm bored stiff and sick of the sight of it.'

The young William kept turning over in his mind the words of the old sailor and at last he decided to make a change and give up seafaring. When he signed off the ship *Pilar de Larrinaga* he sought a job ashore and promptly got one. But the new job and the change did not bring happiness. He found it hard to settle and decided to take up flying. He paid £3 an hour for flying lessons at the Surrey Flying School, a lot of money then, but he thought it worthwhile. However, an instructor said to him one day: 'You're wasting your money here, you know. Why don't you join the Royal Auxiliary Air Force and get paid while learning to fly?'

This William Hickson did, joining No. 601 Squadron as a rigger. The squadron then had Hawker Harts and Hawker Demons, biplanes with a lot of rigging work. As a rigger, after doing a job on an aircraft, he had to fly in it and the young man got in plenty of flying hours. It also taught him one way of being sure of doing a repair properly, but he thoroughly enjoyed himself. This was, however, too good to last and came to an abrupt end with the outbreak of war in

September 1939. Soon after, he appeared before the Tribunal and reported to *HMS President.*

William Hickson also looks back on the voyages he made in the *English Trader* before she joined convoy EC90 for her fateful last voyage. He first sailed in her as gun layer in January 1940. From Southend she joined a convoy for Freetown and then steamed to the River Plate.

During this voyage across the Atlantic, they had a scare when with a convoy. In fact there were many scares, but this had a touch of humour. William Hickson, standing on the gun-deck, spotted through binoculars a small pole protruding from the water. It had a white wake showing that it was moving. It was only a few hundred feet astern of a freighter. Hickson immediately telephoned the bridge but the officer in charge was so incoherent with alarm that he gave no order. The gunner should not have fired without a definite order from the bridge, but the matter appeared so urgent that he took it upon himself to open fire. He felt sure it was a U-boat creeping up on the unsuspecting steamer. He manned the gun himself and fired two rounds at the target. When the firing stopped, signal lamps clattered urgently from ship to ship and the suspected 'raider' turned out to be a fog buoy. The threatened freighter's bo'sun had decided to try out a buoy and should have given notice to the convoy Commodore so that neighbouring ships knew what was happening. The fog buoy consisted of a barrel with a spout. It was towed well behind the ship in convoy providing the following vessel with a useful marker in poor visibility.

Hickson was worried at the consequences of having taken it upon himself to open fire without a definite order. But he was, in fact, commended for his instinctive and prompt action in taking no risks.

One day, on the return voyage to Britain carrying a cargo of grain for Aberdeen, the gun layer was chatting with the third mate – a survivor from the *Titanic* disaster. Seated on No. 4 hatch cover enjoying the sunshine the officer said almost casually: 'I shall not live to see England again.'

William Hickson looked at him in amazement and scotched the idea but the third mate insisted and took a nip from a whisky flask saying that he knew his own feelings best. The gunner thought the incident so unreal he forgot it, but a few days later when the *English Trader* was lying off Aberdeen waiting to unload, the first mate hurried to Hickson with a very serious look on his face. He was much upset and said they had just found the third mate dead in his bunk. He had died in the night. His premonition had come true.

In October 1940, the *English Trader* with John Elliott as third mate, sailed from the Firth of Forth with a cargo of coal bound for the River Plate. She had taken on an almost fresh crew and was going to sail right round the north of Scotland. In the North Atlantic they struck extremely bad weather which split the convoy and the escort protection. All the time they were being hunted by U-boats. The escorts did their best, dashing about after elusive contacts, scattering depth charges like chicken corn. It was a miserable voyage for all; the ship was rolling and pitching, continually battling with heavy seas; the men were hardly ever able to get out of wet, cold clothes and being on watch with few breaks, they were dead tired. The misery of being soaked to the skin and keeping watch hour after hour in almost mountainous seas, when nearly dead-beat can be experienced but not imagined.

The master, Captain Harkness, hardly left the bridge. Sightings of submarines were constantly being made by various ships. Several vessels were torpedoed. The remaining ships were eventually told to make the best speed they could and proceed independently. The captains bore the anxiety and tenseness for days on end hardly knowing sleep until they were well clear of the danger area. Usually on a ship at sea, there is always someone sleeping and someone waking but during this time hardly anyone had time for sleeping. That time of strain applied to almost all the crew and William Hickson certainly had no opportunity to sleep in his pyjamas!

The *English Trader* was still dogged by trouble although this time not from the enemy. In his cabin one day, Hickson was startled by a terrific clatter below him in the ship. He dashed out and soon saw the captain and mate hurrying up along the deck – the rudder was not responding to the helm. Anxious examination showed that the rudder-post had come right out of its bearing and the rudder was useless. This misfortune may have been due to the terrific battering the vessel had taken in the wild North Atlantic storms. It left the ship wallowing and an easy prey to any U-boat that might find her.

News of the trouble was radioed to Freetown and the assistance of a large tug requested. Meanwhile attempts were made to proceed. The bo'sun made up temporary rafts of timbers and by towing these astern on either side of the *English Trader* they hoped to keep her steady. But the strong tides soon proved this useless, the ship yawed violently from side to side. They could but wait for help. While doing so a wisp of smoke was seen on the horizon and shortly after several others appeared. They neared and several vessels were seen around an aircraft carrier. The flotilla came within a four-mile range and then a cruiser came close to signal: 'What ship?'

Captain Harkness signalled back: *'English Trader,'* and also told what the trouble was. The Navy promised to wireless Freetown and then steamed off. Apparently this Force was hunting a lone German raider and the *English Trader* had come under suspicion.

'The following day, still stationary after hours under a colourful sky, smoke was seen again and hopes were raised that a powerful Dutch tug had arrived to tow them into port. It turned out to be a sloop, *HMS Bridgwater*. She attempted to take the *English Trader* in tow, but it was like putting a boy to do a man's work. The tow kept parting. The *English Trader's* bo'sun seemed to spend all his time splicing new ropes. The experiment of using an 'insurance' cable for the tow was then adopted. And once when the sea got up a little, the strain was so great it pulled the bollard right out of the deck of the sloop. The sloop was then employed as a rudder. Lines from the *English Trader's* stern to the forepart of the *Bridgwater* were used to hold the steamer on course. As the sloop moved to starboard or port, she could correct any deviation of the *English Trader*.

Even in this predicament a touch of humour lightened the situation. Just as dusk was falling, the Captain of the sloop signalled his tow: 'Abide with me: fast falls the eventide.'

Had the tow parted during the night, the *English Trader* would have wallowed helplessly till morning. The slow speed made both ships 'sitting ducks' for any enemy raider or submarine, and sure enough a U-boat did appear. It fired two torpedoes at the sloop. They ploughed through the water leaving a foaming wake but passing between the two ships, astern of the freighter and ahead of the sloop. Obviously the submarine commander had not realised that both ships were almost stationary, the tow having parted, and he calculated that the vessels were proceeding at normal speed. The sloop swung round and dashed off in hot pursuit of the submarine. She did not return until nightfall and then without any good news to report.

The day following this near miss, as dawn was breaking, there came a shout from the starboard lookout: 'U-boat in sight!'

William Hickson dashed to the starboard side of the gun-deck. As he did so the bridge ordered: 'Let go everything!'

The tow was immediately cast off and the *English Trader* swung round just as the gun layer was getting his sights on the submarine. The U-boat had obviously been surprised for she was on the surface possibly re-charging her batteries. The gunner re-adjusted his guns, then just as he did so the *Bridgwater* moved directly between him and his target completely screening it. The sloop had opened fire but the range was so close she could not depress her guns sufficiently and the enemy craft crash-dived below the water. Possibly the U-boat crew was more scared than the British sailors for the submarine did not appear again.

As the tug did not arrive, the labouring sloop helped the freighter all the way into Freetown. Here, divers spent some days repairing the rudder. It was Christmas 1940. Then, laden with a cargo of coal, the steamer once more set out for the River Plate. But when a few hundred miles into the Atlantic trouble struck again.

Hickson happened to be looking for'ard from his gun-deck, when he noticed a blue vapour coming out of the ventilators. He reported this to the mate on the bridge. An immediate and anxious examination, made by a man with breathing apparatus, showed that the coal in No 3 hold was alight. Furthermore, checking the other holds revealed that all four holds were on fire and also the fuel in the ship's bunkers was burning. It was a highly unpleasant situation. The ventilators were promptly sealed and the holds more tightly clamped down to prevent air getting to the burning fuel. The risky decision was then made, rather than return to Freetown, to proceed on the 3,000 miles still to go to reach the River Plate.

The following days were horribly unpleasant; the fumes from the burning coal seeping from any crack in the holds, became almost overpowering. To move along the decks the crew had to keep to windward, and at night, sleep was almost impossible as the choking smell got into every corner of the ship. In addition, the heat from the checked but unquenched fires in the bowels of the vessel made the decks so hot the steel plates began to warp.

At last, with great relief, they steamed into the River Plate, but as there were no fire-fighting appliances at Montevideo they had to proceed upriver to a small village where fire tenders came alongside and poured water through the ventilators into the holds. All was going well until there was a sudden and heavy explosion. It shook the ship from end to end and the steel hatch-boards were flung high into the air. One steel length struck the second mate on the shoulder, tearing open a long gash and flinging him to the deck. He was hurried ashore for hospital treatment and rejoined the ship at Buenos Aires some days later.

Apparently the water poured on the burning coal had formed gases resulting in the explosion. The holds were eventually cleared of the cargo, now more coke than coal. The ship then loaded grain for Britain.

It was whilst loading grain in a dock at Buenos Aires that William Hickson fancied a walk by himself into the city. There were few people about when he saw three sailors approaching. He knew they were not British for they had ribbons dangling from their hats and he wondered if they were Norwegian. He was in civvies, as British sailors were not allowed to wear uniform in the port. As they came nearer, he realised that they were three members of the *Graf Spee* crew which lay scuttled in Montevideo harbour and her crew had been interned in Buenos Aires. They should not have been out in that town. He decided to walk on as casually as possible, but they recognised him, looked him over from head to foot and then spat on the pavement. One barked out: 'Bah, Englander!' William Hickson kept going.

The temperamental 'Lady' then started for Freetown, rolling steadily on her 6,000 mile journey with thousands of tons of grain in her shopping basket. No lights were allowed on deck and they had strict orders if they saw any other vessel to avoid it.

At his stage of the war, with a keen shortage of escorts for convoys, many vessels had to be routed independently, but it was highly dangerous. The convoy system, which eventually helped to win the 'Battle of the Atlantic', proved that protecting a group of ships with destroyers, corvettes and aircraft, was the best means of defeating even the U-boat 'wolf packs'. Of all ships lost at sea by enemy action in the last war, 72 per cent were sailing alone.

In March of that year, 1941, the U-boats lost three of their aces, *Prien* (who had penetrated Scapa Flow defences and sunk the battleship *Royal Oak*),

Schepke, and *Kretschmer*. This stunned the U-boat command, and the summer of 1941 was a time of comparative quiet in the North Atlantic. But there was plenty of submarine activity in the South Atlantic still.

So, making for Freetown, the *English Trader* was very much on the alert. When three or four hundred miles out she was informed that the *SS Benvenue* had been torpedoed some 150 miles ahead of her. Would the captain keep a sharp lookout for survivors – and of course – the U-boat! That meant the area of the attack was some 18 hours' steaming time ahead of them. Shortly before dark, Captain Harkness told his officers that they were nearing the vicinity of the torpedoing. William Hickson was on watch on the gun-deck, and just when he wondered if the light was too bad to pick out any object such as a lifeboat or raft, he saw through his binoculars a stick-like object four miles or so away. He informed the bridge, and the captain said they had also spotted two masts of lifeboats in a different direction. He told William Hickson to try and keep his eyes on his sighting.

It was difficult, and dangerous, to stop and pick up the two lifeboat crews as the ship would be stationary and a good target if the submarine was still around. The two lifeboats were crammed with men and despite appeals and calls from the *English Trader's* loud-hailer, they would not approach the steamer. It took a lot of bad language from the captain to make them eventually come alongside, and over 30 seamen climbed up the scrambling nets. One of them was the *Benvenue's* gun layer and later William naturally took charge of him, straight away asking: 'Why on earth didn't you come aboard when we first hailed you?'

The survivor grinned. 'Well,' he said, 'we saw you rolling as you approached and thought you were a German supply ship with a cargo of torpedoes.'

He knew that torpedoes make a heavy cargo, and only a small quantity can be loaded – and the half-loaded ship rolls.

'Oh,' said William, 'that is the normal condition with us.'

Unfortunately, while these men were being picked up, the ship swung with the tide and William Hickson was unable to hold onto his original sighting. The light was fading. He told the captain, who circled but was unable to locate the other lifeboat. Finally, the *Benvenue's* captain who had come aboard said: 'It's too risky. We're inviting the U-boats to attack. Push on, and send a message to Freetown.'

The next morning a Sunderland flying boat passed over the ship. Less than an hour later, the plane again approached and signalled that they had found the third lifeboat and rescued its crew.

When the *English Trader* reached Freetown, William Hickson was talking to one of the survivors of the third lifeboat and asked him what had happened. 'Why didn't you send up flares?'

The seaman explained that when they left the sinking *Benvenue*, a case of rum was put into their lifeboat to be shared among the three boats, but they got parted and the crew of that boat were left with all the liquor. After being in the boat several hours they thought they were so far from land there was practically no chance of them being picked up, and they might as well die happy with the rum as not. So, the bottles were opened and most of the men were so drunk they did not know what was happening around them. They were fortunate indeed to be picked up by the flying boat.

All the crew of the *Benvenue* were thus saved except one – the radio operator. At the last moment, as they were leaving the ship he realised they would need an auxiliary radio transmitter in the boats. He went back to get it and returned as the last boat was lowered. Despite the pleas of his mates in the boat, he would not jump, crying out that there were sharks in the water. Tragically, he went down with the ship.

The *English Trader* left Freetown for Leith and arrived on June 26th, 1941. All the crew signed off including Captain Harkness; he was being promoted to be master of the *Scottish Trader*.

The new crew which signed on at the shipping offices of the company were a truly tough bunch.

The freighter set off for Cuba, joining a slow convoy. They followed the normal route round Scotland and the *English Trader* was chosen as the Commodore's ship. An elderly, retired Naval high-ranking officer came on board with a Yeoman of Signals and staff. The convoy included some old Canadian riverboats which could not do more than five knots. This reduced the speed of the entire convoy. The Battle of the Atlantic was at its height. The ships followed the standard zig-zagging pattern and had the protection of a Catalina aircraft, as well as destroyers and corvettes. The Catalina gave aerial protection as long as possible, then radioed the Commodore that she must now leave and the convoy would proceed without air cover.

On the morrow, a report was received of an enemy aircraft approaching. The gun crews were warned and the gun layer saw the aircraft appear. He identified it as a Focke-Wulf Condor and promptly notified the bridge. The officer on duty was scanning the plane through binoculars and told the gun layer that it was a Catalina. William Hickson was quite unconvinced and called upon Dan – who was something of an expert on aircraft recognition – to identify it. Dan said it was a Condor, so William again reported to the officer on duty that his men were confident the aircraft was hostile. But once more the officer assured the gunner it was friendly. There was some bad language on the gun-deck and Dan said that the distant plane had underslung engines which are not a feature of a Catalina.

However, no one else in the convoy seemed to worry about the visitor. Nevertheless, on the *English Trader*, all the gunners were ready to open fire.

Suddenly the aircraft, circling the convoy, came from astern and flew low over one column of ships. It dropped fire bombs on the steamer immediately astern of the *English Trader*. She was the *Pilar de Larrinaga*. A fire broke out at once on the vessel.

The Focke-Wulf swung sharply away, as it did so a large piece of the plane broke off and the Condor plunged steeply into the sea. With her propellers turning at high speed she was drawn down immediately so that only the foam and wash of the impact was to be seen. Apparently, the *Pilar de Larrinaga* was flying either a protective kite balloon or used her PAC weapons and the attacker flew into the steel cable and destroyed itself.

The two *English Trader* gunners had been unable to fire as the aircraft was so low. The enemy plane was too far away on the perimeter of the convoy for the ships to open fire until it made its run in from astern of a column. If the gunners had opened fire they would have hit the ship astern of them or the destroyer. It was a clever run-in on the part of the enemy pilot.

This Condor however, had done its work for the flames on the steamer spread rapidly and eventually the ship had to be abandoned. The convoy's rescue ship picked up all her crew.

After the war William Hickson put the sea and its perils behind him and built up a small joinery and decorating business in a Hertfordshire town. Today, having reached retirement age, he relaxes and just does the jobs he feels inclined to tackle. This mostly means helping elderly folk who cannot afford big repair bills, or looking after some of his 'good customers' of earlier years. Whatever contentment retirement brings him, he has earned it.

He is a kindly man, not embittered by the long years of hardship, nor what he saw of bloodshed and suffering in World War II. Sometimes, in his workshop he gets drawn into reminiscences of those grim years, but as with so many other men, the haze of time envelops the events, they take on an air of unreality so that a man almost questions if they did really happen. But the smell of planed wood, paint and linseed oil has replaced the scents of the sea and the exotic or foul smells of foreign ports.

Slim built, five feet ten inches tall, with unusual green eyes, he still enjoys good health. His crop of hair is now tinged with grey, mostly due to his age, but a little maybe, has been caused by his experience on Hammond Knoll during those awful nights way back in 1941.

Very occasionally he misses the song of the wind in a ship's rigging; the chuckling and gurgling of a changing tide against the vessel's hull; the mewing of gulls and the sight of an albatross gliding on wide wings in a ship's wake in the South Atlantic. And there was the comradeship of the sea – a pipe and a yarn with a shipmate while their vessel lay at her moorings on a sunny day.

Sometimes the memories almost take on the haziness of unreality. He nearly questions: 'Did I really see the torpedo's wake as it just missed the ship's stern?'

'Did Johnny die at his gun?'

But, as for his two nights on Hammond Knoll – well – there is the tin of State Express 333 in his joiner's shed. It's real enough. And the old lifejacket lamp in his first-aid box.

He had half-emptied that cigarette tin as he sat squeezed into the flag locker with his arms pinned to his sides, but just able to get the soothing cigarettes to his lips.

Time strides on. The *H F Bailey* and *Louise Stephens* have long since been replaced. Henry Blogg and Charles Johnson and most of the lifeboat crews who went out on that service, are dead. George Mobbs became coxswain of the Yarmouth boat for several years and retired in 1966. He lives at Gorleston and keeps many interests in the sea including a small sailing boat.

Out in the North Sea on Hammond Knoll, the corroded remains of the *English Trader* are undoubtedly there, buried by many feet of sand and continually washed by the moody sea.

What does live on while memory lasts is firstly the magnificent spirit of Joe Biss taking a joking farewell of his shipmates as he raised his arm and shouted: 'Taxi! Taxi!' knowing his last hope of survival had gone when the sea snatched the raft from his grasp.

Secondly, the exemplary courage of the 20 lifeboatmen who would not accept defeat even at the hands of such a furious sea.

And lastly, the amazing courage of Britain's merchant seamen. Many, having spent days on a freezing sea in crowded open boats, were rescued and after survivor's leave, went back to another ship enduring the sea's anger and the enemy's malice with matchless fortitude.

Notes

1. The *English Trader* had originally been the *Arctees* and was built by the Furness Shipbuilding Company Ltd. of Haverton Hill-on-Tees in March 1934, to the order of Sir Joseph Isherwood. Sir Joseph was a noted naval architect who invented three types of hull contruction; the longitudinal framing method, the bracketless method and in 1932, he patented the Arcform method. This, as the name suggests, meant the hull was built as an arc. Viewed from astern or ahead it still formed an arc. In those competitive years, Sir Joseph believed this type of vessel was more economical to operate, and he put his faith into practice by ordering three vessels on his own account from different ship builders. He named them the *Arcwear, Arctees* and *Arcgow*. The *Arctees* was registered under the ownership of the Arctees Shipping Company Limited, and was managed by Isherwood Arcform Ships Limited.

The Arcform design was not taken up widely by shipbuilders although tankers to this design were produced in the United States, but the advent of war probably halted further development of the system at that time.

The *Arctees* was bought in 1936 by the Trader Navigation Company Limited, London, who renamed her the *English Trader*. Her gross registered tonnage was 3,953. With an overall length of 374 feet and breadth of 57 feet, her depth (which was all important for what happened in this story) was 23 feet 6 inches. Her engines, made by N E Marine Engineering Company Limited were triple expansion 357 NHP. She had two single-ended boilers with a working pressure of 220 lb psi.

2. The first lifeboat was stationed at Bamburgh in 1786, when Lionel Lukin converted a Norwegian yawl into a lifeboat. And since the foundation of the RNLI in 1824, its crews have rescued 106,500 (31.12.80) lives. Not every mariner knows that the Lifeboat Service is manned by volunteers. On 26th October 1941 the men manning the boat had not been conscripted nor detailed to do this work. Seven of them had, in fact, raced to the boathouse to 'claim a

lifebelt' – for men still competed for a place in many crews, not for what money it would bring but for the honour of serving in such a gallant company. A lifeboatman commanded respect in the community where he lived.

A large proportion of lifeboat calls come from inshore fishing boats. At times the most capable seaman and fisherman needs help outside his own craft and skill. This applied particularly in wartime. So most seafaring men – and these included the lifeboat crews – put the odd coin in the RNLI collecting box with no thought that they one day would need the services of the Institution – but there was always the other fellow. He might need the lifeboat; they contributed to help him!

3. Readers will be interested to compare the near disaster that befell the *H F Bailey* with the remarkable and much more recent experience of the crew of the Kilmore, County Wexford, Eire Lifeboat on Christmas Eve, 1977. Young Joseph Maddock, acting second coxswain, was twice washed overboard and recovered into the boat on each occasion. The 37ft Oakley self-righter *Lady Murphy* was on a mission in storm-force winds in some of the worst seas of recent years. A long period of hard south-westerly wind had fetched up a very heavy swell into the Western Approaches and high seas were created right across the area from the Irish Coast to Cornwall. The *Lady Murphy* took a tremendous sea on her quarter and was capsized. She righted herself in seconds. Her crew restarted the engines but Joseph Maddock was washed out of the boat on that capsize, but recovered. When the boat was again turned turtle, four of her crew were swept into the sea. including Joseph Maddock. Three of the men were recovered, but one man lost his life.

Joseph Maddock said: 'On the first occasion my greatest fear was that the lifeboat wouldn't come back to me. First of all, I thought that there was nobody else left in the world but myself, that everybody else had gone. So when I saw the lights coming on the boat, I think I came back to life. But on the second occasion I was quite close to despair. I thought the boat couldn't come back a second time . . . On the first capsize . . . when I went underneath I wondered which way up I was. The lifejacket worked perfectly. It was only a matter of seconds and I surfaced. I gave a few shouts when I came up to see if there was anybody else in the water.

'Two things ran through my mind: Should I kick off my boots or keep them on? If I'm heading for the rocky shore I would be better with my boots on my feet. So when I saw the lights coming up on the boat – they probably were on all the time but the boat had gone quite a distance away from me – I kicked off the boots and held on until Tom – Coxswain Thomas Walsh – headed back up to windward again. When I thought he would be close enough to hear me I gave a few more shouts. So they took me on board.

'My brain seemed to be racing very clearly. I didn't think I had a brain until that night! I was thinking of so many things. I thought: Christmas Eve, terrible night for something to happen. What will they think at home? Will the boat come back for me? Will I kick off the boots? Will the lifejacket keep me up? Should I swim for the fender – I saw one off the boat and stayed very close to it because it looked bright in the water. It was all over in a few minutes.'

Few lifeboatmen have been swept overboard twice on one service and survived!

Coxswain Thomas Walsh was in command of the *Lady Murphy*. When Coxswain Walsh was asked by Captain Roy Harding, Trials Officer of the RNLI – who had himself been a coxswain and had experienced a capsize – about the problem of getting a man out of the water and into a lifeboat, he agreed that even in a modern lifeboat with very little freeboard, the difficulty is great.

He said: 'We were so short of manpower the second time' – four of his crew had been swept overboard. 'With four in the water it left only three on board. I never thought it was so hard to get men back into a boat . . . You not only have the man in the water, but you have chaos on board as well. Your mast is down and fallen across on the side; there are stays, there are aerials; your plastic canopy is down round about you and you can't get near the wheel without picking it up to climb in under. Your movement on deck is very restricted, even to go to the help of anyone.'

The Cromer boat, of course, did not go right over so the men remaining on board did not have the same confusion to contend with – the tangle of gear, aerials and a collapsed canopy.

The same question was put by Captain Harding to Coxswain George Dyer of the Torbay station who had lost a man overboard on the night of 19th February 1978, in Lyme Bay. His boat was the Arun class 54 ft steel lifeboat.

After the sea that hit them had rolled his boat onto its beam-ends, washing a man out of it he said: 'The second coxswain took the wheel and I went aft because the second coxswain isn't a big man. The biggest of us went aft to keep the tow clear – we were towing a pilot boat – and bring the man in the water aft to where there was more arm room. It was a problem of weight. The guard-chain tended to foul our lifejackets, and then we had got to lift a tidy bit of weight about four feet, I should imagine, plus a bit of motion. We didn't like that because I could see that the man had hurt his arm. We tried to push him off until the right sea came to bring him in all in one go.'

On Christmas Eve 1977, the same night as the Kilmore boat turned over twice, the St. Ives boat *Frank Penfold Marshall*, also a 37ft Oakley class self-righter was knocked down onto her beam-ends after being hit by a gigantic sea.

Both coxswains were asked recently if they had any forewarning of the exceptionally high seas which caused the trouble. Was there any change in the pattern of the seas? Was there any appreciable increase in the wind?

Coxswain Thomas Cocking, Senior, of the St Ives boat said: 'There was no forewarning. None whatever.'

He added: 'We were outward bound, 17 miles north of St Ives when we got a recall – red flares off Porthtown. We came back – oh – six miles. On the way back the boat behaved beautifully. We were all happy with her. We were singing carols. We were nine miles from Portreath when the second mechanic who was on my starboard hand shouted: "Look out, Tommy!" and then when I looked, there was the sea just rolling up. It completely covered the boat right over. We were going along full speed. The next thing she was just picked up and we were on our beam-ends. I held the wheel as tight as I could. I was holding on to the binnacle so that I had the wheel spoke held hard against my wrist. The wheel couldn't move. I thought I kept her straight.

'When we came out of it the second coxswain said: "Tom, I can't see any lights."

'I said: "Eh? They aren't there!" And that boat had literally turned on her port side a hundred degrees. And we brought her back. It seems ages when you're on your side going along like that. Endless, and you're saying to yourself: Now is she going? Then up she comes. Thank God for that, men!'

Coxswain Thomas Walsh of the Kilmore boat said in answer to that question: 'It took us completely by surprise. No doubt of it. There were pretty big seas running all right, but there was no heavy breaking water whatsoever. We had come for miles and we had seen nothing like that. Then we seemed to come on a wave that was just coming to the point of breaking and we just rolled with it and went right over. It must have picked us up under it. There was no sound at all.

'Then the noise started coming like breaking water, in – around – and under the boat. She had run on it. But the minute she started running she was toppling at the same time. You know when a wave comes on the break how the head curls over? We must have gone right over with her.

'Jimmy Bates, former coxswain of the *Lady Murphy,* was out on the corner of the pier watching and afterwards he asked: "You didn't go end over end, did you?" I suppose he had seen the navigation lights and then they went down and disappeared and he could see the stern light. But actually, we didn't. We went to port. You could feel her rolling over. But to him, looking from a distance away it seemed that we had gone end over end.

'The second time I could hear the wave breaking, coming down on us but we hadn't time to bring her up to this one either. I gave her full ahead on the starboard engine to bring her up to the weather. The wave was coming at us from port.'

Coxswain George Dyer of the Torbay lifeboat station had been out on 19th February 1978, in the Arun class 54ft lifeboat *Edward Bridges.* His boat too, had been knocked down by an exceptionally heavy wave in an east-southeasterly storm which had followed a long period of high winds so that conditions in Lyme Bay were really bad. The very big sea which broke right over the Arun's flying bridge was estimated to be $30-35$ feet high with an additional 12 feet breaking top. One man was swept overboard but he was recovered. Coxswain Dyer agreed also that the wave which hit him was a surprise.

He said: 'It was so slow it took us by surprise. You'd never think it was going to happen. She went over so slowly we were all looking at it laughing. Then a couple of seconds and up she came. Beautiful. It was the topping that knocked us over. We had a pilot boat in tow but she was up on the top of it. We had the worst of it, I should imagine. When we were looking up aft as you do, she looked as though she was coming down with us as we went. But when the pressure of water came off and the lifeboat came up, everyone – even the bloke who had been washed overboard, seemed to come with us . . .'